Trompe L'Oeil Today

Ursula and Martin Benad

Trompe L'Oeil Today

for Painters, Interior Architects, and Homeowners

Translated by Ingrid Li

W. W. Norton & Company
New York • London

Picture Credits

Archiv Wolf–Christian von der Mülbe, Dachau: 66, 127, 1331, 148, 155; Atelier Benad, Munich: pages 2–3 and figures 3*, 15, 16, 18, 22–33, 35, 36, 38, 43–46, 48–51, 54, 56, 58, 59, 64, 65, 67–71, 73–82, 84, 85, 96–99, 103, 108*, 126 (*from U. and M. Benad: *Illusionsmalerei*, Ravensburg-Urania, 2000); Atelier Fabienne Colin, Arcueil: 114, 156; Amblard, Pascal, Paris: 93, 94: Arnild, Susan, Ebeltoft: 53, 55; Bayrische Staatsbibliothek [Bavarian National Library] , Munich: 130: Berghuis, Jan, Gravenhage: 39, 40, 52: Breslich & Foss Ltd., London: 7, 19, 60 (with permission of Breslich & Foss Ltd from *The Painted House*, first published in London by Macmillan London Ltd, © Graham Rust); Biswanger, Claus D., Munich 4, 6, 87–89, 91, 138; Bobin, Jean-Claude, Nanterre: 149, 152, 154; Deutsches Theatermuseum [German Theater Museum], Munich: 14; Francis, Ron, Macclesfield: 100–102, 141–143; St. Anthony Franciscan Monastery, Garmisch-Partenkirchen: 2; Friedrich, Reinhard, Berlin: 147; Grand Illusion Decorative Painting Inc., New York: 41, 42, 47, 57, 72; Guégan, Yannick, Quimiac: 115, 118, 163; Haas, Richard, New York: 122; Horsman, Bill, Boston: 8; IPEDEC, Pantin: 5, 128, 150; Keimfarben, Diedorf: 111; Lecce, Athos, Via Giuriati 7, 20129 Mailand, Italy: 86; Leistner, Dieter, Mainz: 10, 90, 109; Mauss, Peter: 106, 158; Müller, Susanne, Munich: 92, 104, 105, 110; Moroni, Lucretia, New York: 9, 61, 62; Ohst, Rolf, Wangels: 11, 37, 113, 120, 121, 161; Pertl, Thomas, Höslwang: 21; Rampp, Karl, Nesselwängle: 1, 12, 63, 107, 112, 160; RML AG, Grünwald: 20, 119, 125, 153; Rust, Graham, London: 117; Schambeck + Schmitt, Munich: 145, 146; Schank, Terry, Sarasota: 123; Schwarz, Christoph, Munich: 34; Vigini, Nicola, San Antonio: 95, 132; Wood, Shona: 83; Zuber & Cie, manufacture de papiers peints et de tissues, 28, rue Zuber, 68171 Rixheim Cedex, France: 13, 17 (both wallpapers are still manufactured and sold by Zuber).

Pages 2–3: Theater decoration in tempera from 1900. It shows lively brushstrokes and can be seen from great distances because of its strong contrasts.

Copyright © 2002 by Deutsche Verlags-Anstalt GmbH, Stuttgart München
English translation copyright © 2004 by W. W. Norton & Company, Inc.

Originally published in German as *Illusionsmalerei Heute: Für Maler, Innenarchitekten und Bauherren*

Library of Congress Cataloging-in-Publication Data

Benad, Ursula.
   [Illusionsmalerei heute. English]
   Trompe l'oeil today: for painters, interior architects, and homeowners / Ursula and Martin Benad; translated by Ingrid Li.
       p.   cm.
   Includes bibliographical references.
   ISBN 0-393-73130-8
   1. Decoration and ornament—Trompe l'oeil. I. Benad, Martin. II. Title.

NK1590.T76 B4613   2003
751. 7'3—dc21   2003052742

W. W. Norton & Company, Inc., 500 Fifth Avenue, New York, N.Y. 10110
www.wwnorton.com

W. W. Norton & Company Ltd., Castle House, 75/76 Wells St., London W1T 3QT

0 9 8 7 6 5 4 3 2 1

Contents

1. CONTEMPORARY TROMPE L'OEIL 7
   About This Book 7
   Pro and Con 9
   Client and Artist 13

2. USING TROMPE L'OEIL PAINTING 19
   Four Categories 19
   Are There Traditional Models? 21
   Functions 23
   A Picture That Does Everything 29

3. INSPIRATION FROM ANTIQUITY 31
   Timelessly Modern 31
   First Style 32
   Second Style 32
   Third Style 33
   Fourth Style 34
   The Surreal as a Design Element 35
   Sweet Decadence 39

4. FROM CROCODILE TO CORRUGATED TIN:
   THE IMITATION OF MATERIALS 41
   The Art of the Faux Finish:
      How to Improve on Reality 41
   Marble and Wood 44
   Snakeskin, Elephant-hide, and
      Corrugated Tin 46
   Tiles and Mosaic 50
   Wallpapers, Drapes, and Carpets 51
   Summary: Modern Faux Finishes 53

5. A WORLD OF LIGHT AND SHADOW:
   GRISAILLE 55
   It's the Form That Counts 55
   Light and Shadow, Bright and Dark 56
   Imaginary Moldings and Architectural
      Elements 57
   Low Reliefs, Busts, and Statuary 60
   Elegance and Understatement 62
   Overview: Grisaille Today 64

6. NICHE PAINTINGS: SMALL-FORMAT TROMPE
   L'OEIL 67
   The Art of Self-limitation 67
   Formal Criteria 68
   Content Criteria 71
   Summing It Up: Big Effects in Small
      Spaces 75

7. A ROOM WITHOUT BORDERS: PAINTING IN
   PANORAMIC FORMAT 79
   Inside and Outside 79
   Creating Depth with Color and Line 82
   Volume: Light and Dark 84
   Distant Views: Proportion and
      Composition 88
   Conclusion: Opening the Wall—
      Suggesting Space 93

8. YOUR POINT OF VIEW: PERSPECTIVE 95
   The Art of Seeing Through 95
   With the Eye of the Spirit 99
   The Geometry of Real Space and Its
      Continuation in the Picture 101
   Mobile Viewers and Picture Design 102
   Conclusion: Best Uses of Perspective 105

9. MATERIALS AND TECHNIQUES 109
   The Fresco Technique 109
   Mineral Colors 111
   Casein Paints 111
   Tempera Paints 112
   Acrylic Paints 112
   Tints and Emulsion Paints 113
   Oil Paints 113
   Airbrushing 113
   Portable Grounds 113
   Industrial Production Methods 115

10. THE PSYCHOLOGY OF DECEPTION 117
   Illusionistic Painting: Art and Life 117
   Murals and Photographic Wallpaper 120
   Imitation, Representation, or Creation? 121
   From Perception to Participation 122
   The Secret Presence of the Artist 124

BIBLIOGRAPHY 125

LIST OF ARTISTS 128

1. Contemporary Trompe L'Oeil

1 *Transformation: waking or dreaming? One reality leads to another, and the visitors of this hotel's swimming pool landscape are spirited into the mountains. (Karl Rampp)*

About This Book

For centuries trompe l'oeil played an important part in the history of interior decoration. This has changed, in part, because fine arts and illusionistic wall decoration developed in different directions during the course of the twentieth century. Today many people consider trompe l'oeil kitschy and simply too much, and they are often insecure in their evaluations, particularly when it comes to contemporary works.

On the other hand, there is great demand for murals that create atmosphere, regardless of their artistic qualities. During the seventies, murals in hotels and private settings were rare, but today both public interest and support are common. Still, it is often unclear what standards can be expected, or how to judge the quality of a painting. Clients and artist often do not speak the same language, and sometimes patrons are not aware of the available options.

This is the starting point of our book. It gives an outline of the diverse possibilities of illusionistic painting and focuses on common projects such as indoor swimming pools, restaurants, and private residences. We distinguish four categories: imitation of various materials, grisaille, small trompe l'oeils, and panoramic murals. These four styles correspond to specific needs and situations. Detailed explanations of materials, technique, perspective, and other topics of interest will be of practical help to the planner and the artist.

This book was written for
▌ Designers and artists who are working in illusionistic styles or would like to develop such a style and need practical suggestions and information.
▌ Interior architects who would like a comprehensive outline of what can be done with illusionistic paintings.
▌ Potential clients who plan to commission a work and need to form an opinion on the quality of a painting or a proposal.

7

❚ Decorators who wish to utilize illusionistic paintings to create a new and different ambiance.
❚ Connoisseurs and artists who will use the paintings in this book as inspiration for their own work.

Pro and Con

Illusionistic paintings are popular. Much can be said in their favor, and one does not have to be an art historian or a salesperson to see why. The reasons for the attraction are obvious:

Pleasure for the senses (figure 2)

A painting executed with love is food for the senses and the soul. Even high-tech buildings reveal the child in the architect wherever playful innocence challenges the supremacy of white rectangles, glass, and steel. Children always love make-believe paintings; the human eye demands pictures!

Practical use (figure 3)

Illusionistic painting can expand the boundaries of even a small and windowless room and make it appear spacious. Closets can be winter gardens, indoor swimming pools can be airy spas—all through the magic of paint. And what's more, the architectural problems of a room can be counteracted, the oppressive effects of a structure minimized. A concrete ceiling can turn into blue sky, wide and open.

3 Of practical use: The painting transforms a small, windowless room into an African savannah. The glaze of the surrounding walls blends into the drawn-back tarps. (Atelier Benad)

Appeal (figure 4)

Illusionist paintings bring color to your walls, in different shades or from the entire spectrum! Color psychologists say that a room's decoration has to contain the "whole spectrum" if only in the smallest amounts, and the colors will harmonize with each other and have a soothing effect on body and soul. It is rarely taken into consideration how the colors of a trompe l'oeil painting influence human perception and even our bodies in a subtle or subliminal way.

4 Appeal: The lush coloration of this loggia combines warm, cool, and neutral hues in balanced harmony. (Claus D. Biswanger)

Fascination (Figure 5)

Trompe l'oeil means fooling the eye. Illusionistic painting is a play with reality and illusion, which invites the viewer to question established modes of seeing and structures of perception. Trompe l'oeil paintings are feasts not only for the eye, but also for the mind.

Transformation (Figure 1)

One could say that a large mural that redefines the optical boundaries of a room creates a new reality. It transforms the experience of viewers and changes their perception of time and space. No ordinary picture in a frame can have such an effect.

6 Personality: The "dream" of a passionate mountain climber. The image of the Matterhorn contains a hard-to-find hidden picture. (Claus D. Biswanger)

7 Individuality: This ceiling fresco impresses with sophisticated perspective, subtle yet contrasting rich colors, and forceful composition. (Graham Rust)

5 Fascination: The artist opens an imaginary space by creating several contrasts. The polarity between monumental architecture and delicate figures, for instance, could hardly be more pronounced. Beyond the dark columns the landscape fades into light and airy distance. Drapes add movement to the static foreground, a billowing gown in the background seems to charm the wind. (Pascal Amblard)

PERSONALITY (FIGURE 6)

Illusionistic paintings can create an ambiance tailor-made to the client's personal circumstances or history. New York or the Caribbean, the Matterhorn or the moon, archaic ruins or surrealist fantasies—all styles are possible, all dreams can come true. No other form of decor or furnishing can have the same psychological impact.

INDIVIDUALITY (FIGURE 7)

Illusionistic paintings are made by hand and carry the artist's personality. What's more, they are unique and direct expressions of human creativity, fundamentally different from printed wallpapers, posters, and other reproductions.

REPRESENTATION (FIGURE 8)

Technically and aesthetically convincing paintings define the style of the space. They speak of artistic flair and original taste. Who would not want to welcome visitors in such surroundings?

But dissenting voices should be heard too:

TROMPE L'OEIL MEDDLES WITH ARCHITECTURE.

Let's face the facts! A wall is a wall and should look like one. Who dares to abuse it by treating it as a canvas!

TROMPE L'OEIL IS MAKE-BELIEVE.

What business does any grown-up have to see paradise where there is none, or to flee reality for an imaginary world?

TROMPE L'OEIL IS ANACHRONISTIC.

A century's worth of "modern art" is a century of revolutionized viewing habits, of searching for a new understanding and new approaches to art. The expressive possibilities of trompe l'oeil were exhausted between the time of the Renaissance and the nineteenth century. We have seen it all; no one is interested any longer in this outdated technique.

IT'S JUST DECORATIVE.

Illusionistic painting is trivial, superficial, ostentatious, and tiring to look at. It clings to simplistic representation and naturalism; it stands in the way of progressive thought.

8 Representation: This imposing painting can be found in the lobby of the Merrimack Building in New York. It covers an area of 4,305 square feet (400 m²). (Richard Haas)

Many more arguments pro and con could be made, but eventually it comes down to personal taste and basic points of view. Everyone has the right to choose what they like, and how they want to live.

Opponents of illusionistic paintings should, however, consider the following points. Many a purist hides a lack of creativity and a stunted joie de vivre behind slick surfaces and anonymous materials. Opposition to trompe l'oeil often comes from an aesthetic reductionism that borders on the neurotic. One adores the blue of Yves Klein or Mark Rothko's color fields, one absorbs monochromes as if they were revelations, and, of course, they can be. But sensual pleasure and the true enjoyment of life flows from other wells …

A caveat for enthusiastic advocates of illusionistic painting: Style is always a question when a mural is to be integrated in a structure. Stylistically uneven, superficial, or kitschy solutions are as questionable as amateurish productions that try to pass as "naïve." There are no established standards for the quality of impressionistic paintings, and the level is often frighteningly low, often for a lack of good examples. A mural can be of such low technical quality that it will pass only as colorful decoration, but will not evoke illusionistic effects. In the long run it will become tiresome unless one has a singularly sentimental attachment to the represented object and no longer perceives its stylistic flaws.

But woe to the hapless visitor who declares the gaudy walls oppressive.

Client and Artist

For a long time illusionistic painting in private homes was the privilege of a small elite. The patterns of communication are therefore not nearly as well developed as, say, between car dealers and their customers. There is prejudice and much miscommunication. Here are some of the clients' hesitations:

My space is not big enough.
This is not a problem at all. Many trompe l'oeil works are commissioned precisely because rooms are uncomfortably small. Windowless baths and dark back rooms with low ceilings are ideal candidates for a transformation through painting. Rooms of generous proportions can become larger and more impressive still.

It's only for rich people.
Any artist, of course, likes to work in a space that is really beautiful, and many examples in this book attest to that. Nevertheless, your own castle is not a prerequisite for a painted view from your dining room. Consider that any other form of decor, be it wallpaper, wall treatments with fabric or other fine materials, or a hung painting, also costs money.

My house painter can do this too.
"And what do you charge per square foot?" It is possible, of course, to price murals as one would price a plaster job, wall-to-wall carpeting, or a new brick face, but even those can be executed with

Criteria	Range of Stylistic Possibilities	
Appearance	• Calm, timeless motifs • References to eternity (ideal landscapes, ocean) • Watercolors (light, airy) • Objects are represented in a highly realistic way (linear elements, sharp edges, concise shadows dominate)	• Dramatic scene that represents activity and actuality • Impasto (thick and dense paint) • Objects are represented in an ethereal way (painterly elements dominate, romantic atmosphere)
Aesthetics	• Commercial decoration (mural design), appealing images for a wide public	• Individual expression (artistic will) • Aesthetic pleasure
Level of detail	• Theater decorations, stylized, hard contrasts: to be viewed from a distance	• Classic trompe l'oeil style, detailed. Subtle nuances and transitions: to be viewed close-up
Historic models	• Stylistically close to "classical" models, e.g., academic landscapes of the eighteenth or nineteenth centuries	• Imitation, inspiration by "isms" or stylistic trends of the twentieth century

9 *Illusionistic painting on a floor: This elegant rendition of marquetry was done for a consulate building. The deception is perfect. (Lucretia Moroni)*

10 *Illusionistic painting on a ceiling: When the castle of Saarbrücken, Germany, was rebuilt and redecorated, the playful approach of the baroque was translated into modern language. (Architecture and painting: Gottfried Böhm)*

more or less skill and in different styles, and the price tags will vary accordingly. No one ever goes out to buy "a car"; one buys a certain model of a certain brand. There is no systematic way to represent the multitude of contemporary illusionistic painting. Every artist develops his or her own approach, which might include a particular style, choice of subjects and composition, and way to deal with the entire space. The chart on page 13 shows a sample of opposites and figures 9–11 illustrate how incomparably diverse the work of contemporary artists is.

Showing off.
"Just one of my little designs . . . ," said the visitor and handed over his card. It was immediately clear that the "design" came from a well-known contemporary trompe l'oeil, and the image on the card was not a free interpretation of it, but a photocopy! Whole portfolios can be like that. The hapless client may not be familiar with the international literature on the subject, and the artist, who claims to have done a lot of work in "the emirates" or "Europe" has an easy game impersonating more successful colleagues whose work has already been published. Even glossy brochures are not necessarily a guarantee of high-quality work. Images of murals can easily be enhanced digitally: an arch out of a book on Italian architecture can be scanned and superimposed on a painting that might in reality be no larger than a sheet of paper. Even if the work was never actually done, the image suggests otherwise and implies skill and experience.

11 Ocean waves. The subject easily becomes cliché, but here it creates a powerful atmosphere. (Rolf Ohst)

12 *An original motif: Cretacean flora and fauna above
and below water. (Karl Rampp)*

A real fresco.

The word "fresco" alone conjures up visions of high art: Pompeii, Giotto, Renaissance palaces, the Vatican, baroque churches . . . Very few contemporary artists, conservators among them, work in true fresco technique, applying water-soluble pigments onto layers of fresh plaster, but a large number of "frescoes" are printed on paper or canvas, aged with modeling clay, manually supplied with patina, and pronounced unique originals. Closer examination of a "fresco" often reveals acrylic paint on a white wall, or on canvas or paper, which was then glued to the wall. True fresco technique is highly demanding and requires great skill and experience.

13 *Panorama wallpaper, "Vie de Brésil," detail. Up to 2,000 different printing blocks can be necessary for the semi-mechanized production of panorama wallpapers, yet they are more economical than tapestries, and began replacing them after the beginning of the nineteenth century. (Manufacture Zuber, Rixheim)*

2. Using Trompe L'Oeil Painting

14 *Theater and illusionistic painting were always closely related. Greek theater is considered the origin of illusionistic representation of architecture, and stage sets have inspired murals since antiquity. In 1918 the famous theater designer Simon Quaglio created a watercolor set for a production of Mozart's* Magic Flute *in the Hof- und National-theater in Munich. These decorations create an open space, typical of the era's fascination with fantastic Egyptian themes.*

Four Categories

Illusionistic painting is a type of realism. By means of paint it simulates a substance, a structure, or a scene on a flat surface. Within the context of the surrounding architecture the resulting image appears to be real instead of painted. Wall, ceiling, furniture, or floor are no longer perceived as ground or support—objects underneath the painting—but the observer identifies them with the image itself. There are four main categories of illusionistic painting, each the subject of a chapter in this book:

▌ imitations of material (faux finishes)
▌ grisaille
▌ trompe l'oeil
▌ panoramas

Imitations of material recreate the optical qualities of things. Grisaille makes the three-dimensionality of an object visible through the use of light and shadow. Classical trompe l'oeil depends on the expressive qualities of the chosen motifs and still lifes—it is essentially iconographic. Panoramic paintings define an expanded space, making new levels of reality accessible to the viewer. The categories are organized hierarchically, the higher ones include and build upon the accomplishments of the lower.

None of the terms used are precisely defined, either in technical or in general usage. To avoid misunderstandings, some commonly used words are explained here.

The French-English term *faux finish* is often used all over the world to describe the imitation of different materials.

Art historians use the term *grisailles* to denote paintings in various shades of gray. The practice of grisaille was originally developed during the fourteenth century as a form of book illustration, but was soon used on wood panels and walls as well. Strictly speaking, grisaille describes the representation of miniature statues and figurines in niches or wall recesses, and it suggests illusionary spaces through graduated shades of color—all on the pages of a book. Later the word grisaille—painting

15 "*Landscape with Ruins*" by Pierre Patel, ca. 1646–47, detail (Louvre, Paris). Masterworks like this view of Arcadia are excellent role models for contemporary painters of illusionistic themes. This panel, originally a decoration for a hotel, impresses with light and dark contrasts and reflections, as well as the contrast between decaying monumental architecture and the tiny figures that enliven the scene.

in gray—was applied to any monochrome representation of subjects like low reliefs, trophies, stucco, trompe l'oeil window frames, columns, or other architectural elements.

In this context the term *illusionistic architecture* should be mentioned. This term really should only be used for panoramic depictions of three-dimensional architecture, like those we see on the walls of Renaissance and baroque palaces. Illusionistic architecture is more than paintings of, for example, stucco reliefs: it is the smooth transition between the real and the seemingly limitless imaginary architectural space.

The term *trompe l'oeil* can also be interpreted in different ways. Decorative painters consider it the representation of three-dimensional ornamentation in grisaille technique, or the imitation of stucco or architectural elements. As a category of fine art, trompe l'oeil developed from architecture

that was painted on the outside of triptych panels and eventually became a subject matter in its own right. Artists of the twentieth century went beyond the ever-popular niches, bulletin boards, hunting trophies, and the like, and stopped at nothing to surprise the viewer with painted curiosities such as pickled embryos or power drills on panels that could be viewed independently from the rest of the room in which they were displayed. The represented imaginary world is complete in itself and can be hung on the walls of any gallery.

From here it is only a small step to the concept of *illusionism*, which includes more than trompe l'oeil: it is the deceptive imitation of reality. Trompe l'oeil is a particular form of illusionistic painting, but not every illusionistic image aims to make the viewer believe that the represented object is real.

16 *"Gallery with Motifs from Ancient Rome" by Giovanni Paolo Pannini, 1758 (Louvre, Paris). Like a stage set, this imaginary gallery is framed by a green curtain. A busy group of copyists draw from the wealth of classical forms. The painting demonstrates how the eighteenth-century enthusiasm for archeological research inspired a renewed interest in the arts of antiquity.*

The term trompe l'oeil is often used freely and interchangeably with the term illusionistic painting, and can thus include all four categories above. Both terms are sometimes wrongly applied to anything painted on walls or furniture that elicits associations with real objects, independent of the quality of the work (for example, illusionistic painting with stencils). True illusionistic painting only exists where illusions arise about the reality of the represented object. Unless artistic skill and integrity are at work the result is often little more than painted decoration or illustration.

The term *panorama* is self-explanatory. In this book we also describe as panoramas the space-opening painted architecture on the ceilings of baroque churches. These paintings "magically" remove entire walls or ceilings, so it seems justified to list them in this category. There are, of course, huge stylistic differences between baroque illusion-

istic architecture and an airbrushed dream beach in an indoor swimming pool, and the term *monumental* simply does not apply in a room with a height of 7 feet (2.5 m).

Are There Traditional Models?

When trompe l'oeil specialists are asked, "Do you have historical models for your work? Do you stand in the tradition of European fresco painting?," they often answer, "There is no connection. All building situations are different from those in earlier centuries, so are the materials, the requirements, and the wishes of the patrons. Early murals almost always show figures within landscapes or buildings. Today the landscapes themselves are the main characters, there are rarely any people in them, historical, mythological, or divine. And

17 *"Drapery Josephine, Red." Wallpaper imitating decorative fabric. (Manufacture Zuber, Rixheim)*

finally there is the maxim: "Finish quickly, do it cheaply." In the past it was decided relatively fast who should get the commission, then the artist had months, if not years, to finish the project. Today clients take months to choose an artist, who is then expected to be done by yesterday.

Even if today's architectural, societal, and aesthetic conditions are unique, nobody can deny the influence of the past. Any painter has learned from the examples of the great masters. Painted architecture has existed since the time of ancient Greece.

Andrea Pozzo was the first to transform flat ceilings into imaginary domes (see figure 130, page 98); Mantegna opened his domes to the heavens; the Mannerists discovered the terraced view of the ocean; and the charms of decaying ruins have been known for more than three hundred years. Illusionistic painters are also indebted to the eclecticism of the nineteenth century and owe many inspirations to it. During this time trompe l'oeil artists developed numerous excellent wallpaper designs. Particularly noteworthy are the French

18 Detail from "Drapery Josephine, White." Because of technical requirements, this print shows clear borders between color areas instead of soft, painterly transitions. This hand-printed wallpaper is in production today.

panoramic wallpapers, known for their unrivalled effects and limited color palette (figures 13, 17, 18). The exotic decorations of nineteenth-century stage sets can be a source of inspiration as well. It should be noted that the architectural forms that were new to the twentieth century are rarely useful as models for illusionistic painters. Should they depict highway overpasses instead of Greek columns? Even "picturesque" subjects such as the cast-iron orangerie shown in figure 8 are no longer in production today.

Functions

One of the many forms of illusionistic painting can be applied in even the most contemporary or minimalist architectural context (figures 19–22). To understand how many different functions such paintings had in the past it is best to look at some examples, and we will do just that, not with the precision of a historian, but with practical interest of a designer who selects whatever seems useful for the task at hand. We may not live in Pompeii or in Napoleonic Paris, but who says that the blueprints for our new house cannot reveal the dreamer or the emperor in us?

MAKE-BELIEVE BUILDING MATERIALS

The imitation of marble was already known in ancient Greece. Sometimes the technique was used to mask less valuable building materials; sometimes the real thing was simply not available at the site, or could not be used for structural reasons. Real building materials were often imitated in areas of interior space that are so high up that the eye could not distinguish painted stucco from original stucco (see figure 74, page 59). The effect is the same; the savings are significant. Imitation stucco in churches plays yet another role: the trompe l'oeil architecture, particularly if applied to ceilings, creates a space that seems to defy gravity and transcends the limitations of the physical world. The paintings can represent a metaphysical reality as no actual building materials ever could.

IMPROVING PROPORTIONS

Improving proportions is one of trompe l'oeil's main functions. Small rooms can appear wider, low ceilings can be raised. A baroque interior (figure 127, pages 94–95) with a ceiling height of "only" 30 feet (10 m) may need to be raised to achieve harmonious proportions, or a room with a simply unsatisfying architecture may need to be reinterpreted through paintings.

GATES TO A DREAM WORLD

Of course the paintings in Pompeii had representative and decorative functions, but they also led the viewers into an imaginary world and diverted them from their daily routines. There are the idealized realities shown in the garden scenes that we find in the families' private quarters. A modern visitor to those sights might feel the transformation even more intensely than the original inhabitants, who were used to this style of decoration. Dream worlds are places where different levels of reality and consciousness interact and follow their own logic. The dreams appear crazy because they seem so real, yet they represent a reality different from the physical world we are accustomed to; they belong to the realm of the soul.

Today, paintings in the Pompeian style are often used independently of the dream theme to create atmosphere and antique ambiance in Italian restaurants (see figure 34, page 37).

LONGING AND DESIRE

Universal themes are subject to the constant changes of "fashion." At the beginning of the nineteenth century scenic wallpapers and the development of a bourgeois way of living made the pursuit of such fantasies possible in private homes. Murals often express such longing in these themes:

▌ the past, antiquity
▌ the distant, the unreachable
▌ the authentic, the true
▌ the wish to be someone else

19–22 Four examples of sky murals painted on ceilings.

19 Design for the vaulted ceiling of the archbishop's chapel in London's Lambeth Palace (1988). A continuous landscape combines the different segments of the vault and shows motifs from all five continents. Different light situations are depicted; night sky leads to sunrise and illustrates the theme, "Christ illuminates the world." (Graham Rust)

We all know the already classic yearning for Venice, Arcadia, or for far-away lands and people. Illusionistic painting offers many settings for such imaginary travel; it can act as a screen for psychological projections. It also plays a role in the increasingly popular photography movement of the nineteenth century, and provides alpine peaks or antique architecture as background for portrait shots. Today's escapist fantasies seek alternate identities in cyberspace and role playing, and state-of-the-art hotels continue the tradition of illusionistic backdrop paintings in wellness oases that simulate complex settings.

Sources of strength

We all have certain images and situations that have particular importance and that we love to recall. The contemplation of an illusionistic painting that reminds us of such things can contribute greatly to a person's well-being, and can even have therapeutic effects.

Subject matter plays a role when it comes to harmonizing living spaces, through Chinese feng shui, for instance. There cannot be any doubt that one feels very different under a low ceiling of dark wooden beams than under one that has been opened up with "heavenly" shades of blue.

Teaching aids

In the late Middle Ages painted church walls were known as "bibles of the poor" and illustrated biblical stories with well-known signs and symbols. In the spirit of the Counter Reformation, baroque churches used trompe l'oeil architecture to expand spaces toward infinity and invited angels and saints into the here and now. While the heavenly beings come close to the viewers' physical reality, the viewers themselves seem to enter other spheres.

20 Fine dining under an illusionistic sky where Pulcinel-
los are having fun on a stone balustrade. The painted sky
dramatically alters the perception of the ceiling, exemplified by the chandelier, which seems to hang from an unlikely spot. (Rainer Maria Latzke)

In profane contexts, too, murals have educational or political functions, although historical paintings and works with a distinct political message, such as the Mexican murals or images of social realism, do not usually employ illusionism.

Contemporary illusionistic paintings are generally free of didactic or political messages, but the reign of agitational illusionistic realism is still unbroken in the fields of advertising and the mass media, where images are multiplied in endless succession. When it comes to filming, photographing, and marketing products, no expenses are spared to present them in the most seductive and favorable light possible, to make them desirable.

Self-promotion

Not only despots like Nero or kings like Louis XIV basked in the glory of their extravagant palaces; the church also used spectacular paintings to demonstrate its wealth and power to the faithful. But representation is not restricted to public buildings. Politically savvy businessmen in ancient Rome were already eager to show their fellow citizens that they could afford the best and had discriminating taste. "Who are you?" and "What do you represent?" are not new questions. Illusionistic painting has always played a role in this context.

Theatrical performance

Illusionistic painting and the theater share a long history from antiquity to the beginning of the twentieth century. While an imaginary reality is presented on stage, society's game becomes reality on the other side of the curtain. Rooms of any house can become stage sets through the magic of illusionistic paintings, fabric coverings, and other props. Guests can enjoy such rooms in vacation settings and play their allotted parts, usually one that is far removed from everyday routines. The subtly aesthetic *Gesamtkunstwerk* (total work of art) of earlier centuries has turned into an artificially orchestrated theme park.

Luxury items, decoration, fetish, artwork

The following four functions are not limited to illusionistic painting, but are often intimately connected with it.

▌ "Painting the town red." Indulgence and luxury afford the same pleasures now as in the past. Too much is never enough, and painters make a living off it.

▌ Illusionistic painting is always a form of decoration, and depending on the period different decoration schemes can be identified. We simply suggest that this decorative function is fulfilled if the product looks good, pleases the eye, and fits. It fills

21 An old barn has been converted to a modern restaurant space. The client wanted to preserve the charm of the dilapidated structure, so the perfectly smoothed and sanded ceiling has been transformed into an inside view of the old barn roof.

a void, meets an expectation, and does not necessarily have any deep meaning.

▌ The fetish function is on a different level altogether, and the label is applied in a tongue-in-cheek manner. The paintings in the caves of Altamira and in the sealed tombs of Egypt are not illusionistic, but they speak of a magical consciousness that can be traced down to the present. These paintings have to do with magic spells; they are not dead objects but have a living connection with the represented being that appeared in the image. Power over the image meant power over the thing itself. In other words, the hot rod in the garage reappears as a model on the nightstand; the departed lapdog keeps watch as an illusionistic portrait. We are looking at relationships that are magical at their core—the picture becomes a cult object. Assertions of power and ownership towards real objects can be experienced and realized by looking at the picture. A Stone Age relic?

▌ To be a "work of art" means here that a painting is beautiful in its own right; it is a pleasure to look at. Even if "noble beauty" is not an official trait of art any longer, it is still the reason for many a commission of an illusionistic painting, which means a work of art.

to be dazzled by the magic of illusionistic painting, to be uplifted, or to bask in luxury.

Today there is no equivalent for such a monumental synthesis of artistic rejuvenation, self-expression, display of splendor, politics, and religion—certainly not in the field of illusionistic painting. Maybe the first computer-animated movie that features "human" characters will constitute a comparable accomplishment. Why? Because the computer simulation of human actors seen by millions of viewers around the globe will be a quantum leap that equals the discovery of central perspective in art. Both deal with imaginary worlds, with the synthesis of many art forms, with esoteric subjects, with marketing, and with the effect on the population at large. Is it possible that the spirit of baroque illusionistic paintings could be expressed in new and surprising ways?

A Picture That Does Everything

In 1685 Andrea Pozzo began to decorate the Jesuit church St. Ignatius in Rome, and pulled out all the stops. A real dome could not be built for two reasons: there was not enough money and it would have cast a shadow on the library of the Dominican Friars next door. But a dome over the crossing (the intersection of the nave and the transept) was considered indispensable, and so Pozzo created a painted simulation. He designed the image of a dome with a decentralized vanishing point, painted it on canvas, and glued it to the flat ceiling. This innovative and daring plan was an inspiration to generations of artists after him and ensured him lasting fame (see figures 130 and 131, pages 98 and 99). Three years later the entire ceiling vault was scheduled to be repainted. Against considerable opposition, Pozzo had all the stucco work removed and painted monumental illusionary architecture that rose heavenward in glorification of St. Ignatius. The patron saint of the Jesuits seems to be present physically and the work emphasizes the special status of the Order and the location. The message is not just narrative, but highly political. Besides, a painting of such imposing scale speaks of wealth and power: who else could afford monumental works of art? The composition and the perspective of the painting also suggest a sequence in which the viewer should contemplate the image on the ceiling, and invites active involvement. A round marble inlay in the floor marks the best viewing position. Paintings, sculptures, music, liturgy, and sermon come together as a great unity, a total work of art. The contemporary visitor is free to come to this space for religious inspiration, for the enjoyment of art,

22 *A painted sky raises any ceiling or opens it up toward infinity. Cloud formations and the quality of light create individual expressions. (Atelier Benad)*

3. Inspiration from Antiquity

Timelessly Modern

Contemporary artists are not the only ones who have been fascinated by Pompeian frescoes. The excavations started 250 years ago and were systematized after 1860. Ever since, it has been fashionable to enjoy revivals of Pompeian design again and again. Louis I of Bavaria had a Pompeian villa; a Pompeian garden pavilion was constructed in Buckingham Palace in 1844; countless Pompeian rooms were furnished during the late nineteenth century. A fascinating mystery seems to lie hidden in the historic murals. The term *Pompeian frescoes* is used here to describe frescoes from Pompeii as well as those from the neighboring towns of Herculaneum, Oplontis, and Boscoreale. The stylistic development of Pompeii mirrors that of Rome even though it became a Roman province under Sulla as late as 80 B.C.

There are four Pompeian styles in Roman painting, and the word *style* is used to describe systems of decoration. The eruption of Mt. Vesuvius in 79 A.D. deposited a 20-foot (6 m) deep layer of ash on the towns and created extraordinarily good conditions for conservation; therefore greater Pompeii yields the best examples of paintings and objects of daily life. The excavations are particularly abundant because the region became popular with Roman nobility after colonization and the rich and famous built luxurious country houses there.

Pompeian frescoes are not really illusionistic paintings, but they contain illusionistic elements. There are imitations of columns and walls as well as other architectural elements shown in central perspective. Nevertheless, we include these paintings in our book for two reasons. First, Pompeian frescoes, regardless of their content, are frequently imitated, and are common inspiration for illusionistic paintings. The surface being imitated happens to be an antique fresco. Second, the formal canon of different styles contains any number of subject ranges: color–line, two- and three-

23 Fantastical architecture in the Fourth Style. (Atelier Benad)

24 *Wall decoration with First and Second Style elements. (Villa of Mysteries, Pompeii)*

dimensional space, imitation–depiction, concrete–abstract, figurative–ornamental. Anyone working with illusionistic paintings will find inspiration here.

First Style
or Structural or Incrustation Style
(ca. 200 to 180 B.C.)

This style (figures 24 and 28) utilizes a method of imitating marble that was already popular in Hellenistic Greece. Walls of relatively cheap material were constructed by simple techniques, covered in stucco, painted, and polished, so that eventually they appeared to have been built from large stone blocks. The walls show three horizontal sections: there is a dark plinth or dado, a section of large sheets or blocks of what appears to be stone, above which are smaller rectangular blocks arranged in horizontal layers, and at the top, a protruding ledge of white stucco. Occasionally there are painted loggias with half-columns of

stucco above the ledge. Door- and window frames and cannelures were also made from stucco and painted to resemble stone. It is unlikely that such decorations were ever mistaken for the real thing, since everyone knew that the stones depicted were not available on site, and that the paintings were simply fashionable. Paint hides the walls and alters reality. Instead of the actual wall, a convincing decoration appears and emphasizes the height of the room in the process.

Second Style
or Architectural Style
(ca. 80 to 20 B.C.)

This style (figure 25) is inspired by Greek theater decorations and was imported by wealthy Romans in their competition to display the utmost in luxuries.

Elements from the First Style were incorporated —e.g., the partition of walls into three horizontal areas—but the elements are only painted, instead of sculpted, in stucco. Views of architecture are added in central perspective—there seem to be columns on pedestals in front of the walls. They divide the middle part of the wall area into three parts and carry architraves, arches, and ceiling elements. This arrangement creates the impression of a three-dimensional stage setup, and the painted columns are related to the actual columns in the room. The middle part of the "stage" usually shows an open door that allows a view of gardens, colonnades, or mythological scenes in a natural setting. Later, the wall areas left and right of the middle also showed such doors with illusionistic views of architecture, landscapes, and gardens. Entire stage sets were represented and life-sized figures acted out mystery plays or appeared in naturalistic scenes.

This style works with two kinds of illusion: representative and imitative. Representative images open up the space to a painted world outside. Imitative realism lets the wall appear as a different architectural element, a façade that allows glimpses of vistas beyond. Sometimes the marble imitations are replaced by plain color fields. Large areas of the walls are painted in red, yellow, black, or white, occasionally in blue or green. Small pictures are presented within those color areas; they stand on painted candelabras or shelves. In the middle of the wall are large pictures framed by temple architecture (aedicules), and here we see the transition to the Third Style.

It is an element of this style and of the Roman attitude in general that mythological scenes restrict-

25 Second Style painting. (Villa Poppea, Oplontis)

ed to public buildings and the palaces of nobility in Greece are now used to decorate private houses. The deeper content of these scenes is often lost, and well-known scenes are combined and reinterpreted as allegories.

Third Style
or Ornamental Style
(ca. 20 B.C. to 60 A.D.)

The Third Style aims for balance and simplicity (figure 26). Emperor Augustus favored neoclassical design with a certain rigidity of form: the period is now called the Augustinian Renaissance. Architecture is represented without great depth and appears mainly ornamental. Freed from the demands of realism, it now stands for tasteful decor and representation. Columns don't support anything; they seem like arms of candelabra or grow like slender stalks. In the upper wall areas architectural paintings are miniaturized and fantastical; in the middle areas architecture acts as

27 *Painting in the Fourth Style. (House of the Vettii, Pompeii)*

frame for the main image, usually a scene from Greek mythology, painted in exquisite quality by a specialist.

The horizontal tripartition becomes a standard framework. Large, monochromatic areas are decorated with filigree borders, ornamental frames, small columns, and candelabras. The friezes appear as marble inlays; miniature paintings show landscapes and figures. There is a preference for lively colors set off by a black or white background. Egyptian motifs are fashionable.

Garden views are a hallmark of the period. Painted in trompe l'oeil fashion, they still appear dreamlike, imaginary, and idealized.

Fourth Style or Illusionistic Style (ca. 60 to 79 A.D.)

During the reign of Nero, attitudes became lenient and increasingly permissive. Life was seen as an endless sequence of amusements, and even the most senseless and depraved or bloody events qualified. Excessiveness and imbalance are also reflected in the art of the time: spectacular displays become fashionable. The earthquake of 62 A.D.

was a prelude to the eruption of Mt. Vesuvius. After the quake many houses had to be restored and redecorated, and the Fourth Style (figure 27) was developed fully.

The Fourth Style pushes illusionism to its limits. Wall areas are still sectioned into three horizontal parts, but background colors become more and more contrasting and intense, and multiple color fields replace unified areas. We see small temples and landscapes, statuettes and reliefs, and their details are rendered with almost manic compulsion—an expression of *horror vacui*? Occasionally the middle section of a wall becomes stage to a play of complicated and fantastical architecture. Multiple vanishing points preclude the impression of a homogeneous space; they are designed to dazzle and confuse the viewer. The central image of the wall decorations are figures, genre scenes, or landscapes set in medallions or floating in mid-air. They are painted in a lively, almost impressionistic manner and use light and dark effects with great skill. Some of the pictures take the form of tapestries or images painted on billowing curtains. The perspective constructions in the upper wall regions become more and more complex. There are strange compositions that defy all rules of gravity and logic. A bizarre and fantastical world is summoned up

30 Illusionary architecture in late Third to early Fourth Style. (Herculaneum)

28 Decoration
from the Villa
of P. Fannius
Synistor in
Boscoreale,
Italy. (Louvre,
Paris)

behind the walls. Atmospheric shades of pink, green, and purple contrast with the white ground that suddenly "reestablishes" the wall. There are still marble dadoes at the bottom, but we also find flowerbeds protected by painted fences. All images are executed in true fresco technique, but the inserted paintings are neither polished nor waxed, unlike the works in all earlier styles. The impression of simultaneously existing planes of reality is enforced even further.

The Surreal as Design Element

Nobody who sees Pompeian frescoes in the original can resist their allure. They strike us not so much aesthetically, but in emotional and intellectual ways. Visitors often exclaim, "They must have been completely crazy!" or "This is totally modern!"

The "modernity" of these paintings lies, in part, in the mix of reality levels, in the evident paradox that cannot be solved rationally, and in part in the combination of apparently contradictory stylistic elements. Here are examples of some possibilities:

▌ Marble imitation or color field? The contrasting fields in figure 28 and the play of light and shadow at the edges give structure and life to the wall and seem to us like prototypes for computer screens. Architectural representation is a mere excuse for the development of an independent aesthetic.

▌ An angel is floating in figure 29, but where exactly? On the wall? On paint? In a black nothing daintily framed by filigree borders? Nearby a green balcony floats above the viewer's head. It casts a shadow, we see it from below, but what is it attached to? The red frieze, which suddenly turns from decorative border into the edge of a building? The black background stretches in front of and behind a window opening. Inside and outside merge. Is this a column or a stalk of bamboo? We are in a fictional world of fascinating mysteries. Secrets, movements, interior and exterior, dream and reality all exist simultaneously.

▌ Figure 30 shows an impossible structure: round on top, angular below, but connected by the same columns. The fictional architecture appears like a vision behind the wall. The wall itself is alive with the contrast of painted columns, color effects, and playful ornaments. In the middle of this ethereal composition, a statue appears, weightless and dreamlike, or is it a man, or a demigod? The figure seems to stand in the foreground of the lightly suggested space, clear sky behind. But wait—the ornament on the left clearly defines the sky as a flat surface, and the picture of a pecking bird seems

32 *Garden scene (detail) from the south wall in the so-called House of Venus in the Shell. (Pompeii)*

33 *Detail of a garden scene in the "House of the Centenarian." (Pompeii)*

left:
31 Theater backdrop: fresco in the Fourth Style in Herculaneum. (National Museum, Naples)

to hang from that same plane. Is this superficial entertainment or magical transformation?

▊ Delicate brushwork fascinates in the "theater set in six layers" (figure 31)—monochromes in the background, lush coloration in front. Even though the lines do not meet in a single vanishing point and the artist did not even apply the perspective of a line of vanishing points that was popular in Greece, the resulting layered space appears thoroughly convincing.

▊ The garden scenes in figures 32 and 33 are rendered so realistically that biologists can identify the birds and plants depicted. At the same time they appear transfigured: A vividly colored sky in the background replaces the receding landscape and acts as an abstract backdrop for the chosen motifs. The scenes are full of life, yet a dreamlike silence pervades.

▊ The mythological figures Mars and Venus seem to have been the models for figure 35, or could they be the master of the house and his lady in mythological costumes?

right:
34 Wall with Pompeian motifs in an Italian restaurant. (Christoph Schwartz)

▊ Pompeian paintings are more than two thousand years old and show many signs of age and decay, yet they seem to us like contemporary creations (figure 36). Undoubtedly, this is one of their many charms. We detect no mediaeval elements, but Renaissance perspective, baroque sensuality, and

35 Mars and
Venus from the
"House of Fate-
ful Love" in
Pompeii.
(National Muse-
um, Naples)

elements of expressionism and surrealism are all
anticipated. Or is it the decadence of the period
that resonates with us today?

Sweet Decadence

Modern designs cover the entire spectrum from the
downright morbid and artificially distressed surface to the perfectly polished appearance that aims
for the greatest possible visual impact of
the image. Figure 34 shows an Italian restaurant
decorated with Pompeian motifs. Figure 37 comes

36 *Painting from the Isis temple in Pompeii. (National Museum, Naples)*

37 Pompeian decoration with inlaid painting. (Rolf Obst)

from a winter garden. The surface's high gloss is reminiscent of lacquer rather than of a fresco. The contrast between the gold ornaments and their black background is the most important element. Dust or any sign of age, whether real or painted, is not desired. The design of the image shown in figure 38 is inspired by the formal and tightly organized Third Style. It was painted directly onto concrete and was distressed with sandpaper. Figure 23 (page 30) is an amusing play with compositions in the Fourth Style without restraints of logic or intellect.

38 Third Style Pompeian paintings on walls and floor transform a balcony on the seventh floor of a high-rise building. (Atelier Benad)

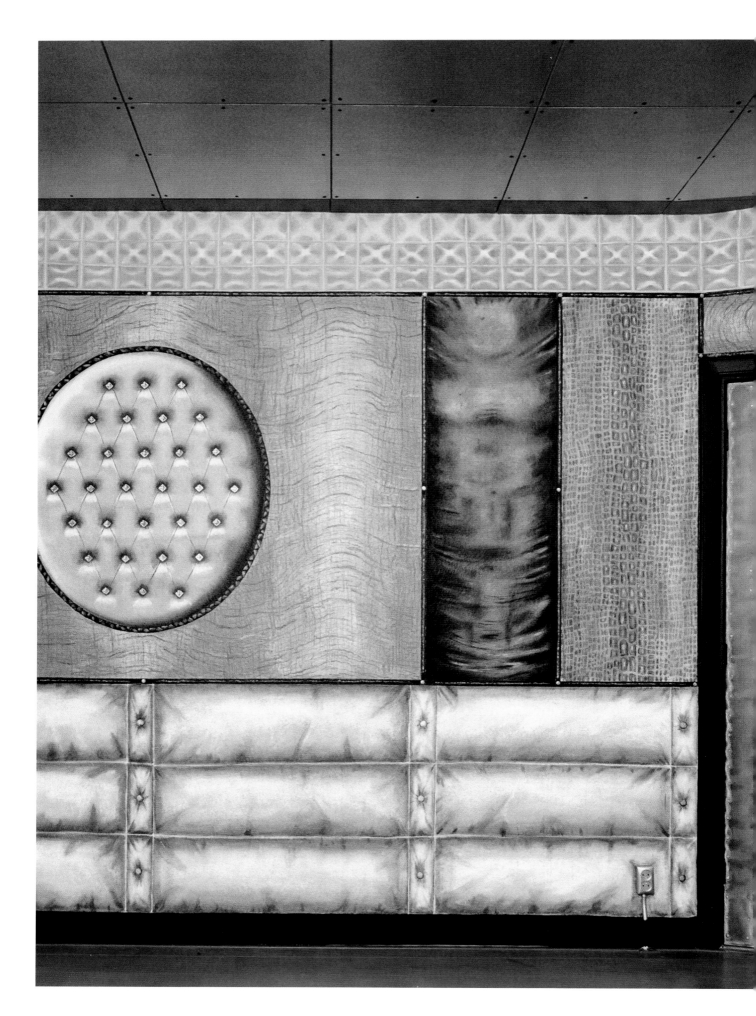

4. From Crocodile to Corrugated Tin: The Imitation of Materials

39 Scene from the "Matrix Room." (Jan Berghuis Jr.)

The Faux Finish: How to Improve on Reality

Imitations of natural substances are all around us. A floor might look like real beech wood, but the effect is produced with printed paper and synthetic laminate. The pudding tastes like vanilla, and we love it, even if the flavor comes from artificial additives. A voice from a microchip makes an announcement and sounds human to us. Hardly anyone objects to things like this. Reality and its surrogates blend; the surrogates take on a reality of their own and define our lives.

Why, then, is there such a fuss when a painter puts a brush to a hollow plasterboard wall and turns it into solid rock?

Unlike the makers of many ersatz products, the painter does not want to deceive, but is only interested in and fascinated by surfaces. The viewer reads them as sandstone, marble, or wood, but a simple touch or tap can clear up the "error" easily enough. Such uncomplicated verification is not usually possible when it comes to aromatic food additives, or when the phone is answered it sometimes takes a while to determine if a real person or just a machine is at the other end. While few people think of chemists and laboratories when they eat vanilla pudding, they usually admire painters and marvel at their technical perfection and skill. The viewers know that they have been fooled; they know they are looking at a painting, and still they cannot help but consider the stone wall real.

Marble and wood are classic subjects for faux finishes, and the tradition is long. Before the end of the eighteenth century there was no distinction between painters who worked on architectural projects and those who worked on panels. The imitation of materials was a well-known craft that was practiced in Europe until the second half of the twentieth century, when it slowly fell into

40 Painted
marble inlay.
(Jan Berghuis Jr.)

41 Painted marble dado. (Pierre Finkelstein)

42 Painted marble with elaborate trim. (Pierre Finkelstein)

43 Painted black marble and three-dimensional gold ornaments.
(Patrice Kreitz)

44 *Silk garment, detail from a portrait of Claude Henri Watelet, 1765. (Jean Baptiste Greuze, Louvre, Paris)*

45 *Ermine, velvet, and silk. Detail from a portrait of Louis XIV, 1701. (Hyacinthe Rigaud, Louvre, Paris)*

oblivion and wallpaper became popular. Today only restorers and church painters have the know-how to create spectacular results with relatively simple means. In England and France the tradition is still alive, and the revival of the craft in many countries since the late eighties is all too often happy with rather mediocre results. The best way to get a perfectly painted "Royal Rouge" (a particularly decorative red marble) is to hire an artist from Paris or New York. The international guild of "faux-finishers" satisfies its clients' demands for perfectly executed surfaces in traditional European style with French or Italian accents. American and British companies have specialized in materials for decorative painters and offer brushes, glazes, and other magical items that an artist elsewhere might only dream of.

Marble and Wood

Magic is a word that can well be applied to the painterly imitation of materials. The painter takes on the role of the alchemist who creates any kind of substance before the very eyes of the amazed audience, if indeed an audience is permitted while the work is in progress. The resulting masterwork can easily outshine the real thing, at least when it comes to appearances. Figures 40 to 43 will substantiate this claim. The appeal can be heightened further if several types of marble are depicted, each with a different structure and coloration. Nuances of white and gray can illustrate the tactile qualities of the material. The painting is usually finished with a high gloss varnish to simulate the perfect polish of the noble stone.

46 *Wood imitation with three-dimensional trim, detail. (Michael Nadaï)*

47 *Wood paneling painted on a sheet of paper. (Pierre Finkelstein)*

Neither the Romans nor the artists of the Middle Ages were quite as sophisticated in their approach. They made honest efforts to mislead the eye, but the viewers were never left in doubt; they always knew that they were looking at an imitation. Marble imitation was a way to decorate large wall areas. Painted marble was not a detailed copy of the real thing, but it was beautiful. It was not until the fifteenth century that viewers wanted painted objects to look realistic. At the same time, the technique of painting with oil was developed. Pigments in oil can be arranged in semi-transparent layers. Soft transitions between light and shadow can be created, and the material properties of the represented objects can be shown in all their intricacies through skillful brushwork and the application of multiple layers of paint. Such subtle nuances and structures cannot be represented in fresco technique, where work has to proceed swiftly and colors tend to dry to opaque films. Prominent Flemish masters of the fifteenth century such as Rogier van der Weyden (1399–1464) or Jan van Eyck (about 1390–about 1441) dazzled their contemporaries with perfect surfaces. In addition, the represented objects often had symbolic meaning. During the following centuries the art of still life developed to

48 *Intricately painted wood inlay. (René Deblaere)*

49 *Study for bamboo painting. (Cepiade)*

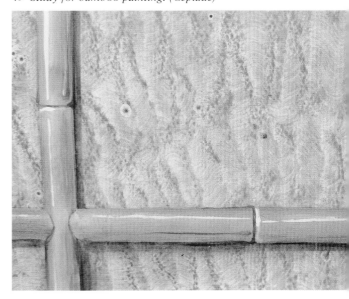

50 *Whitewashed oak carving with lead, both painted.*
(Jan Berghuis Jr.)

Figures 46 and 47 show examples of such flawless imitations of wood. These do not just copy the material itself, however, but also masterly examples of woodwork—delicate moldings and carvings are represented three-dimensionally. Inlays show different types of wood (figure 48). It is hard to believe that this is really painted particleboard, or that the otherwise "real" parquet floor in figure 9 (page 14) was embellished with painted wood inlay patterns.

Marble and wood imitations can also be painted in less ambitious, more stylized versions, and price is not necessarily the issue. Such imitation of materials can be chosen as stylistic and decorative elements that are not really illusionistic. A realistic approach can produce structures that resemble natural stone or wood formations but do not claim to be exact copies. For the decoration of contemporary interiors it is often preferable to suggest materials in this way, particularly on large wall areas. "Real marble" requires great skill and can easily appear ostentatious. If the illusionistic effect is not convincing, the painting can seem gaudy, but a playful "five-minute marble" is a different story altogether.

Snakeskin, Elephant-hide, and Corrugated Tin

Marble and wood are not the only materials that can be imitated. Tried and true recipes for the imitation of tortoiseshell, agate, lapis lazuli, and other rare materials have been in use for centuries. There are no limits to artists' imagination. Each has his or her own tricks and secrets and ways to depict bamboo mats, leather covers, damask, snakeskin, elephant-hide, cow- or leopard skin (figure 49). Mere decoration can become enigmatic artwork as, for instance, in the "Matrix Room" (figures 39, 50, and 51), where elephant and reptile skins and plastic are imitated, and objects seem to be hidden under tightly stretched fabric. We see slightly dusty silver mirrors nailed to the walls, sheets of corrugated tin, lead dadoes, and other fascinating oddities. The room, and the expression of a particular way of life, was inspired by the movies *1984* and *The Matrix*. The same artist takes a different and humorous approach with an illusionistic painting of a wall in a bar (figure 52). Not only did he paint the smoke-stained and torn wallpaper but also the wood paneling, the telephone, the dart board, and, of course, the bathroom doors. More than one slightly inebriated customer has tried to open them.

perfection, and paintings of flowers, fruit, and hunting scenes expressed an interest in careful observation and the wish to copy nature. We use the term *trompe l'oeil* for these still lifes if the explicit intention is to fool the viewer. The eighteenth-century paintings in figures 44 and 45 show an almost excessive pleasure in the sensuality of the painted fabrics. In the same time period we find the earliest images of rare wood, marble, and precious stones that were designed to exceed nature in brilliance and perfection.

right:
51 Plastic on brushed steel? Acrylic on canvas! (Jan Berghuis Jr.)

52 *Trompe l'oeil in a bar. (Jan Berghuis Jr.)*

53 Antique
Spanish tiles,
faucet, and stone
sink are "only"
painted. (Susan
Arnild)

Tiles and Mosaic

Nothing is impossible! Plaster and paint in a bathroom create a more comfortable room climate and a "softer" view. While we use fewer real tiles, muralists outdo each other with imitated ceramics, usually as decor in kitchen areas or in locations other than humidity-prone bathrooms. Paint can function as a virtual replacement for tiles only when it is sealed with a scratch-proof two-component varnish. Tiles in shades of characteristic Delft blue with fine cracks, a yellowish-white background, and irregular joints are a well-known and traditional subject. Other sources are antique Spanish tiles (figure 53) or industrially produced tiles (figure 57).

Wood imitations can focus on flat inlays or three-dimensional moldings and carvings. The same is true for the representation of tiles. Mosaics in particular often show light and shadow around every single stone piece, as well as light reflections and irregular or broken edges (figure 54). Even Michelangelo's frescoes have been translated into painted mosaics (figure 55). Stylized variations can be utilized for large floor areas where mosaic patterns can be applied in stencil technique (figure 56). The gaps between the stones were not painted separately: the underlying floor remains visible between the stenciled stones.

54 Painted mosaic of a fruit-basket motif. (Jeanne White)

Wallpapers, Drapes, and Carpets

Historically we can trace the development of wall decorations in a sequence of fresco, textile drapes, wallpaper made of fabric and, later, of paper. From the end of the eighteenth century such papers were imprinted with textile patterns and draped folds (see figure 17, page 22) or with trompe l'oeil motifs. Those who could not afford silk or printed silk imitations on paper hired a painter, and the results are more fascinating to us

55 Painted mosaic after a motif by Michelangelo. (Susan Arnild)

56 Decorative painting of a mosaic in Pompeian style. (Atelier Benad)

57 Painted imitation of a tiled wall. (Pierre Finkelstein)

today than the originals ever could have been. Every production process has its own parameters, and artists were charged to design the wooden printing plates that were used for panoramic wallpapers to achieve optimal effects. Delicate color gradations and glazed effects were not possible; instead we find precisely edged color fields, subtly and aesthetically matched in their nuances, often in overlapping layers (see figures 13, 17, and 18). Different techniques were used for painting. The silk painting from the early nineteenth century shown in figure 58 combines a variety of effects.

First, a ground of blended red and green hues is applied. This creates a shimmering effect when the piece is finished. Then, a textile pattern is applied with the help of stencils and freehand. The shimmering effect in figure 59 is also created with a ground of blended colors. Finally, star-shaped, irregular stencils are added and seem to reflect the light like glistening fabric. The final touches are roses and butterflies, stenciled and with hand-painted details.

Drapes are another form of fabric imitation and had already been used as decorative elements in

left:
58 Imitation of a baroque silk wallpaper. (Villa Palagione, Volterra)

right:
59 Painted silk wallpaper with flowers and butterflies. (Villa Palagione, Volterra)

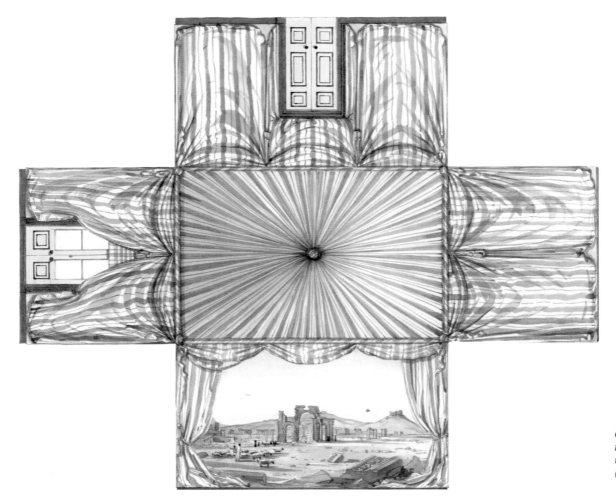

60 Design to transform a room into a tent. (Graham Rust)

61 This carpet is not knotted, but stenciled. (Lucretia Moroni)

62 An interesting aspect of the painted carpet: The structure of the parquet floor remains visible and adds a touch of humor. (Lucretia Moroni)

Roman basilicas and early Christian Romanesque churches. The lower parts of their interior walls were often painted in stylized trompe l'oeil images of marble and draped fabric. This custom is still in use today, in much the same way. Unlike the painted fabric drapes on wall bases, freely arranged draperies usually allow the artist more freedom and individuality (figure 60). Drapes on dadoes tend to be stylized, but those painted on other parts of the walls usually allow the artist a much greater range of possibilities. Folds appear in different sizes, shapes, and materials, and they express personal style.

What would theater decoration be without painted curtains and drapes? When the fire curtain of the Odéon Theater in Paris was restored (figure 149, page 111), it was not just its gigantic dimensions that posed a problem. The paint had to be completely matte and unreflective even under the glare of powerful spotlights. Pigments were suspended in rabbit glue in a time-honored recipe.

Even textile floor coverings—carpets—can be imitated successfully. Figure 61 shows a well-organized work in progress. Stencils are applied and combined to produce the spectacular results seen in figure 62.

Summary: Modern Faux Finishes

Design Variation

- Detailed imitation of sandstone, marble, granite, etc.
- Idealized, hyper-real representation (wood, marble), inlay technique
- Stylized, naturalistic style
- Exotic surfaces, painted tortoiseshell, burl wood, bamboo, leather, etc.
- High-tech with patina
- Detailed mosaic painting
- Mosaic painting / carpet painting directly onto the floor
- Drapes on entire walls or bases
- Freely arranged drapes, sometimes as a frame for murals

Application

- Substitute for materials that are too heavy and expensive or difficult to obtain
- Aesthetic fascination: exceed nature
- Free, lively design that appears natural
- Create exclusive ambience or irritate and provoke
- Create special atmosphere
- Original decoration or fascination with the trompe l'oeil technique itself
- Original substitute for real mosaics or carpets, or to create a design or color scheme that cannot be realized with the actual materials
- Classical approach to wall decoration
- Decoration with individual expression

5. A World of Light and Shadow: Grisaille

63 Quadriga motif, detail from a mural around a swimming pool.

It's the Form That Counts

Grisaille, or monochrome, painting is very much the opposite of material-imitation painting. The subject of grisaille is not precious substances or the beauty of surfaces, and it never depicts any materials for their own sake. The sculptural form in its three-dimensionality is of sole interest here. Grisaille painting shows forms that appear realistic but they are modeled only by gradations from light to dark. Whether the represented statues were made of marble, sandstone, plaster, or wood is irrelevant. Even the very idea that statues might be represented is not necessarily supported.

The seven virtues and seven vices painted on the dadoes of the Arena chapel in Padua by Giotto in the early fourteenth century might look to us like illusionistic representations of stone figures, but it is questionable if such an impression was actually intended by the artist. After all, at the time, actual statues were often painted and gilded. The same is true for grisaille book illuminations of the fourteenth century. It is assumed that the figures painted in frames or niches were not meant to appear to be actual stone statues but that they have primarily symbolic and allegoric meaning and simply represent the figures in a three-dimensional mode. After all, illusionistic paintings make little sense on the pages of a book, and are much more convincing on the outside of altar panels, where painted figures are believable as statues in niches. These painted niches are thought to be the beginnings of modern trompe l'oeil images (figure 64). In the fifteenth century dadoes or whole wall sections were decorated with painted reliefs, busts, sculptures, niches, and other realistic architectural elements. Not only the three-dimensional effect of the figures was considered important, but also the accurate representation of the materials themselves to create the illusion of real architecture. Grisaille painting did not return to its origins until the artists of the baroque period began to imitate stucco, a material that represents form but has no characteristic appearance of its own.

64 *Detail from the right panel of Jan van Eyck's "Ghent Altar," ca. 1390–1441. (Louvre, Paris)*

65 *Modern trompe l'oeil on a church façade in Rome.*

66 *Allegory of Generosity. Detail of a ceiling mural in the Emperor Hall of the castle in Würzburg, Germany. (Giambattista Tiepolo, 1969–1770)*

The "thing itself" (to quote Kant freely), shown for the perfect representation of form, is the ideal subject of grisaille (figure 66).

Light and Shadow, Bright and Dark

The term *grisaille*, or gray-painting, can describe a number of styles: an illusionistic representation of stone sculptures, decorative imitation of various reliefs and stucco work, or the visual structuring of a wall through painted ashlars. Three-dimensionality is suggested through the use of highlights along edges and shadows in joints. Three different shades of gray suffice for the job.

Like all representational art, grisaille painting translates light and shadow into lighter and darker shades of particular colors. The painting does not show the actual color of the represented object but its three-dimensionality, its position in space. Figures 67 and 70 do not show classical grisaille paintings: they are patterns for mosaic floors, but the same principle applies: dark

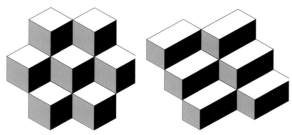

67 a, b Two different patterns for three-dimensional floor mosaics.

right:
68 A distortion of the basic patterns above expands the sense of space even further.

69 Brickwork. A pattern developed from the form of a pyramid with a cut-off tip.

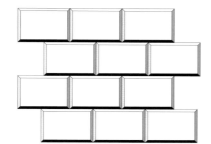

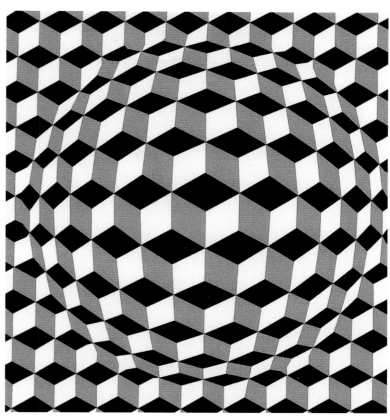

recedes, light advances. The surfaces, of course, don't move but remain right where they are; it is the eye and the mind of the viewer that move. The viewer usually imagines a source of light somewhere at the top left of the object. The lighter parts seem to be directly illuminated; the darker ones lie in shadow, their existence dependent on the lighter ones. Maybe this is why we feel that shadows recede, even though we could just as eas-ily say the same thing of the lighted surfaces if both appear at the same angle in our imaginary space.

It is almost impossible to look at these patterns and not see three-dimensional objects, and it is easy to represent sculptural forms through simple geometric elements. Façades can be decorated with illusionistic stonework according to the same prin-ciples (figures 69 and 71). The familiar frames on your computer screen, if you run Windows or Macintosh, look like three-dimensional frames, and when you click on a button with your mouse you expect the inside of the button to recede as if you had pushed a door bell, or it doesn't look right. In your computer, too, the sun shines from the top left.

Imaginary Moldings and Architectural Elements

Painters of the eighteenth and nineteenth centuries represented architectural elements in elaborate gri-saille technique, and their technical perfection and creativity has been unrivaled since. Figures 73 to 78 show motifs from a Tuscan villa. These neoclas-sical and retrospective paintings are of very high quality, and many contemporary artists copy them and learn from them. Figure 72 shows a systemat-ic overview of various molding types.

70 a, b Designs for tile floors with a three-dimensional effect.

71 a, b This design can be used for door panels or small façade segments.

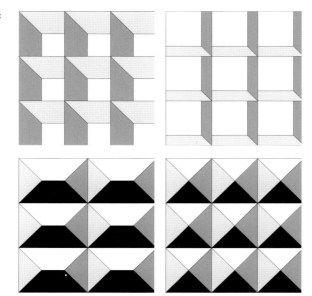

72 This panel was created for educational purposes, and shows how different molding strips can be defined through light and dark shades. (Pierre Finkelstein)

Figure 74 depicts the great hall of Villa Pala-gione, which is decorated almost completely with grisaille. The intricately painted stucco work covers the entire ceiling vault, and the light-dark of the painting is indistinguishable from the hues of what seems to be the color of the represented material itself. Gray-on-gray becomes beige-on-beige, brown-on-brown, or green-on-green. The ochre tones in figure 73 for instance imply the presence of sandstone.

Trompe l'oeil paintings always suggest in a playful manner that we might be looking at the real object or the real material, a claim that cannot be maintained if the viewer is close enough to touch and examine the wall. But stucco painted high up on a wall or on the ceiling cannot be identified as real or unreal. How could one make such a distinction looking at the ceiling relief shown in figure 76?

73 *Painting in the "Gothic Room" of the Villa Pala-gione. (Volterra)*

74 *Detail of the grisaille in the Great Hall of the Villa Palagione. (Volterra)*

75, 76 *Painted plaster work in the Palazzo Viti. (Volterra)*

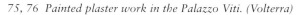

77 *The barrel vault in the entrance area of the Palazzo Viti is painted to resemble a coffered ceiling. The strong contrasts take the actual light situation into account.*

78 *Ring ornaments as expressive architectural detail. (Villa Palagione)*

If grisaille is combined with material imitation of carved, turned, chiseled, or polished items, the effect can be more real than reality because actual lighting conditions rarely bring out details as convincingly as a painting can (figures 79 to 82).

Low Reliefs, Busts, and Statuary

There are many applications for grisaille in figurative art, ranging from decorative low reliefs (figure 85) to images with highly personal statements beyond conventional categories, like the one shown in figure 65 (page 56). This fascinating illusionistic painting on the façade of a Roman church simultaneously deals with the question of reality and the connection between image and reality, since the impression left on the cloth of Veronika was not made by human hands.

The painted statue in figure 84 illustrates yet another aspect of grisaille. It shows neither a real person nor a statue. The depiction of an actual

79 *Small section of the impressive ornamentation in the interior court of Santa Chiara, Naples.*

80 Baroque ornament, detail. (Michael Nadaï)

81 Elaborate rendition of a relief. (René Deblaere)

person might appear too trivial or obtrusive, while a statue could seem too bland. Here, the choice is left to the viewer.

Figures 83 and 63 (page 54) illustrate a further characteristic of grisaille: its subtle and reserved approach to color. If a design should be impressive, even dramatic, yet maintain color neutrality, grisaille is the ideal choice. It respects the surface of the wall as ground and the surrounding architecture as frame, it defines the subject matter without being obtrusive, and it establishes the character of the entire space.

82 The effect of a low relief in this ceiling mural was created in shades of gray and gold. (Versailles)

83 *Panel in warm shades of sepia. (Graham Rust)*

Elegance and Understatement

The studies in figures 87 to 89 show the difference between monochrome and polychrome paintings and a simple white room without color design. The monochrome painting is sophisticated and understated; the polychrome version appeals more to our emotions. By comparison, the unpainted room looks plain and unfinished in spite of the elegant furnishings.

Figure 86 shows a contemporary but classically inspired version of grisaille in the house of an Italian architect. Here the technique is interpreted freely; its appeal lies in the combination of the gray architectural elements and the subtly polychrome figures and beige sandstone walls.

The image in figure 90 is even further from the traditional confines of grisaille painting; it cannot properly be described as such any more. We find neither a material that can be clearly identified, nor an obvious source of light, nor traditional perspective or definition by light and shadow. Even the arrangement, position, and functionality of the columns remain unclear. Nevertheless, the illusion of objects layered in space opens up the actual room and allows the viewer great freedom

right:
86 Interior with grisaille painting. (Giovanni Simonis)

84 *Figure of a nude. (Atelier Benad)*

85 *Painted marble with superimposed grisaille. (Cepiade)*

of interpretation. The result is a semi-abstract illusionistic painting that balances the use of formal vocabulary and representation. The painting was not a later addition to the room but was conceived together with the architectural form of the space, and thus it is part of a long tradition of interdisciplinary architecture and creation.

87–89 Different atmospheres are created in this room with rolled-on white paint, monochrome, or polychrome murals. (Claus D. Biswanger)

Overview: Grisaille Today

Design Variation

- High-contrast light-dark painting with decorative effects

- Realistic imitation of stucco work, architectural details, and reliefs

- Representational paintings in shades of gray or other monochrome nuances

- Monochrome all-round design

Use

- To structure and enliven floors and façades with three-dimensional elements

- To enrich and enhance the appearance of walls and to appeal to the senses. Is it real or painted?

- To quote themes and motifs in a subtle and unobtrusive way, to give character to a room without primacy of the artwork. Self-restraint as a means to heighten expressivity. Speculations about the represented material allow for different interpretations

- To express subtlety and elegance

90 Transparent lightness is the defining element in the concert hall of the Music Academy, Essen. (Gottfried Böhm, in cooperation with Stefan Böhm)

6. Niche Paintings: Small-format Trompe L'Oeil

91 *Living room in a city apartment. To give a space a fresh identity it is not necessary to cover every surface with murals. Carefully composed views in harmony with the specific circumstances can change proportions dramatically. (Claus D. Biswanger)*

The Art of Self-limitation

The history of small and mid-sized trompe l'oeils begins with the simulation of objects in painted wall niches. But this art form never led a niche-existence, and it is still popular today.

In the fourteenth century illusionistic wall niches were already painted on interior church walls, filled with liturgical objects that could actually have been placed there. Later, in the fifteenth century, it was predominantly Flemish artists who painted wall-niches on the outside of altar panels (see figure 64, page 56). When the altars were closed, those everyday objects were visible. Sometimes symbolic objects like roses, skulls, cloths, or other ritual items were depicted. When the altar was opened, the luminous image on the inside was revealed. Painted wall-niches are still popular decorations and are often combined with statues painted in grisaille technique. In the scheme of a surround painting, niches are often added as decorative elements (see figure 4, page 9).

Niche motifs are popular because the shape of the niche also defines the outside edge of the painting. Imaginary niches of a mere square yard (meter) can be painted on any wall; there is no need to design a treatment for the entire surface. The sixteenth and seventeenth centuries added new motifs: wall openings, bookshelves, sills, curio cabinets, bulletin boards, trophies, and more.

Another version of trompe l'oeil is the "picture of a picture." A pioneering example is a fifteenth-century work from the School of Ferrara: skillfully rendered remnants of packing cloth signal that we are not looking at Mary, but at a painting of Mary. An even more subtle treatment of the picture-of-a-picture theme was created around 1500 by the Master of Frankfurt who painted a portrait of his wife and added a life-sized fly to her kerchief, so lively that one wants to shoo it away. But the fly is part of the composition, a reminder of our mortality. Another famous work comes from Cornelius Norbertus Gijsbrecht. Around 1617 he painted a

Formal Criteria

It is almost impossible to list everything that should appear under this heading. Applications vary in technique and purpose, and range from medieval altars to surreal paintings of the twentieth century. Many paintings by René Magritte qualify as trompe l'oeil, but the formal criteria listed below do not always apply to all examples. Nonetheless, this summary is useful because it enumerates all the aspects that should be kept in mind when a self-contained trompe l'oeil is being planned.

▌ We have already mentioned the contour line as a criterion that is met by all earlier examples. This means that no object should appear incomplete because of space limitations. An object may be hidden by other objects, but it may not be intersected by the edge of the painting, otherwise an illusionistic representation is not possible. An artist who paints a jumping frog complete with a puddle on

92 Painted door: Man's best friend. (Susanne Müller)

view of a painting's back side: a wooden frame to which canvas is tacked, a little label with an inventory number. How many visitors to his studio might have turned the picture around only to find that this back side is actually a front? The list of examples is endless. Gijsbrecht's picture opens up a new dimension—the painting becomes an illusionistic object that can be moved in space freely. From then on, he paints half-finished images onto large boards, adds the easel, brushes, mahlstick, his work clothes on a hook, and he cuts the whole thing out along the outline. The resulting moveable object is called *Chantourné* and can include contours of people. Life seems to be a play on a stage set after all.

In the eighteenth century illusionistic images painted on furniture become popular. There are card decks on table tops, as if someone had just interrupted a game; there are painted violins hung on doors, and painted coats "forgotten" on a hook.

93, 94 "At the Beach" was created as an example and combines different elements of illusionistic painting. The figure of the boy is copied from a work by Norman Rockwell. The picture is not a true trompe l'oeil in spite of the realistic representation because objects appear cut off at the edges and do not relate to the surrounding space. In figure 94, "Angela," this connection is created with a stone door frame. (Pascal Amblard)

95 *Wine Cellar. The life-size door could easily be mistaken for the real thing. The interior of the cellar is shown foreshortened. (Nicola Vigini)*

the floor has met these criteria; so has the painter of a garden scene that is bordered by a window or door frame. Such frames are particularly useful for the realistic depiction of landscapes (see figure 94). In figure 93 we see what happens if a frame is missing: the painting is still illusionistic, but it lacks the characteristics of trompe l'oeil.

▌ A further characteristic is that objects must be shown life-sized, or they will not be confused with the real thing (see figure 92). When a space is shown according to central perspective, the size of objects in the distance has to be diminished according to scale (figure 95).

▌ In trompe l'oeil panels, extreme perspectives should be avoided because they necessitate particular viewpoints for the observer if the illusionistic effect is to be achieved. Low reliefs are preferable, and the objects may recede behind the actual painting surface—in the representation of a shallow niche, for example—or they may appear to protrude slightly into actual space in front of the painting. Such reliefs appear realistic from almost all points of view, hence the popularity of painted bulletin boards, all variations of folded or crumpled paper, playing cards, newspaper clippings, and the like. The "picture of a picture" falls in this category, ideally when shown in a painted frame under cracked glass; so does a lizard on a floor (figure 96) or decorative drapes around a door or a window, and none of them will interfere with the laws of perspective (figure 97). The viewer can move around the room freely and the trompe l'oeil appears realistic from every vantage point. For the depiction of landscapes it is best to choose wide angles and to avoid distant vanishing points and linear structures (figure 100). The suggestive power of a perspective construction always requires that the viewers remain relatively stationary in front of the image.

▌ The painter of a self-contained trompe l'oeil usually assumes that it will be examined up close and expects that the viewer will touch the objects to verify their existence (or non-existence). For such scrutiny technical perfection is a necessity. Brushstrokes must remain invisible and colors must be blended smoothly to simulate three-dimensionality. Varnish can provide gloss where it is required. Sometimes it might be necessary to

96 *Lizard and dragonfly. Such motifs can be painted directly on the floor or a wall, but here the stone tiles, too, were painted. (Palm Fine Art)*

paint exaggeratedly sharp contours, black shadows, or linear silhouettes to create an image that is "more real" than reality.

▌ It is important to consider the light conditions under which the image will be viewed, because they influence the design. If there is a window in the room, painted shadows should always match those that actual objects would cast, but it is not necessary to include all details, such as the reflection of those windows in the painted glass panels of a cupboard.

Content Criteria

Many trompe l'oeil paintings are executed on canvas or on boards, which are easy to move around and can be hung in any room or fastened to any surface, but the deception will only be effective if the image is logically related to its surroundings. The depicted objects have to be believable in the particular space. Painted cupboards, bookshelves, medicine cabinets, curio cabinets, wardrobes, and other small pieces of furniture are always a good choice, particularly if their style matches the rest of the furnishings (figure 98). This is also true for painted windows and doors (figures 99–106). The

97 *A curtain seems to be draped over a windowsill. (Atelier Benad)*

98 *The wood inlay was painted around a mirrored wall niche of a sales room, transforming it into an open armoire. Even the lace cloth over the "door" is painted and alludes to the merchandise actually displayed. (Atelier Benad)*

99 *This trompe l'oeil includes the window frame, the sill, and an ashtray, and makes this view of the ocean credible even from a landlocked building. (Murs Dec)*

100 The edges of this trompe l'oeil panel are identical with the edges of the represented window frame. It could create an illusionistic effect in many different rooms or surroundings. (Ron Francis)

101 *Painting on an exterior wall (about 10 x 13 feet [3 x 4 m]). From his office window the client had a view of a plain wall and wanted it transformed into a relaxing sight. Now a Turkish landscape reminds him of his vacations. (Ron Francis)*

illusionistic paintings shown in figures 141 and 142 (page 104) create an almost mystical atmosphere, partially because the contemporary window and door elements of the surrounding building have been represented in original size. The viewer spontaneously considers the window real, so the rather unlikely content of the image becomes an enigma. The two pictures in different locations of the same apartment have yet another effect. In both, the woman is shown in a similar pose. During the second encounter the viewer might think "There she is again!" and enjoy the mysterious reappearance of the image. By the same token the representation of people can lead to problems, since a person shown in a trompe l'oeil can appear frozen in time. This may be appealing to visitors who pass through a room quickly, or if this extended presence is the main topic of the image, as in the example above. But if a trompe l'oeil in an office or a living room shows a servant who offers the same bowl of fruit year-in and year-out, it eventually becomes a tiring caricature.

The criteria mentioned above are necessary conditions for a convincing trompe l'oeil, but not a guarantee. A well-painted bookshelf or a correctly shaded flowerpot might be pretty and might even surprise the viewer at first glance, yet they could be little more than decorative.

The true appeal of a still life or the placement of a trompe l'oeil lies in its relationship to the surrounding room and the people who live there. Every artist has his or her own personal style, and

102 *"Sleepy Hollow" book-shelf: The classic trompe l'oeil motif of a book-shelf is combined here with anamorphic perspective. The gnome appears to jump out of the book when viewed from just the right angle. (Ron Francis)*

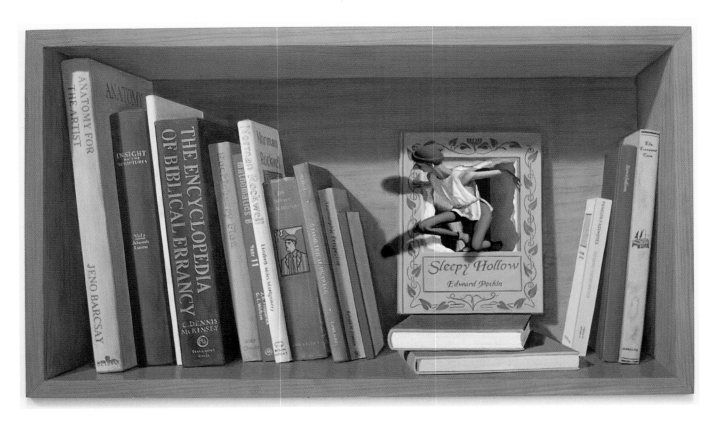

103 Fictional view of a land-scape in Provence, related to the interior space through a "window frame." (Atelier Benad)

besides surprising illusionist effects, the pictures can reveal individual stories. Figure 102 is an example, and it represents much more than just a bookshelf. The artist illustrates anamorphic perspective with the gnome who escapes from "his" book (compare this to figure 143, page 105).

The pictures can also relate directly to the people who live in the space. Bookshelves can become portraits of their owners by the choice of titles, pages open, still-burning cigarettes in ashtrays, and other distinctive accessories. Messages enclosed in trompe l'oeil panels from earlier centuries are frequently undecodable for us today because we are not familiar enough with the daily lives of their original owners. The signature of the artist and the date were hallmarks of trompe l'oeil panels for centuries. Painted slips of paper with other personal information were often added, seeming to stick out from the surface and thus invalidate the illusion of the painting while establishing another illusion, that of the paper. What an intricate deceit! Trompe l'oeil often reflects upon itself and occasionally acquires a didactic component. Views into landscapes usually suggest issues beyond the personal. The walls recede as if by magic, space is created, a view of the sunny side appears. Similar factors define the panorama (figures 91 and 103).

Summing It Up: Big Effects in Small Spaces

The themes of small and medium-sized "self-limited" works of art are different from the themes of large panoramas. But the images of room-expanding views from open windows have much in common with panoramas, as we have already mentioned, particularly if elements of existing architecture are integrated into the painting. Classic small trompe l'oeils give familiar objects of everyday life a special status. They are suddenly imbued with meaning, tell stories, appear paradoxical, or invite self-reflection. Large formats, in contrast, present a room without borders; they often represent ideals such as an idealized landscape, timeless events, or general subject matter. In smaller formats we usually find objects that seem to be situated in front of the painting surface, while the motifs of large works more often seem to exist in a space behind the surface. To simplify, we could say that small paintings focus attention on the here and now, while large ones invite reflection on distance and eternity. A painted niche might depict personal items, such as car keys that the owner is constantly looking for, but they would be misplaced on a column near the ocean. If the patron

104 *Cupboard-turned-aquarium. (Susanne Müller)*

glimpse of a non-existent adjacent room (compare figure 106).

▌ A story should be told, a personal message delivered, a high aesthetic standard maintained. Examples are panel paintings with illusionistic still lifes depicting a range of subject matter from fantastic collectors' items to classical flower arrangements.

▌ The room should appear larger—the wall should be opened up. Examples are large-format works that show views of distant landscapes or representations of distant worlds, idealized in space and time.

still insists on sunglasses or half-emptied wine bottles in a panoramic landscape, they usually do not convince, and seem out of place. Why not let these items tell their story in a small painting all their own?

Small and medium-sized trompe l'oeils appear in many different contexts. Format, use, and material depend on the specific purposes.

▌ The room should be highlighted with an unusual effect. For example, there could be a butterfly or a branch of ivy on an otherwise undefined wall, or a lizard on the floor. Unexpected and surprising effects can be achieved on furniture: A violin seems to hang on the door, playing cards or a photograph to lie on a table, or the cupboard becomes an aquarium (figures 104 and 105).

▌ The room should be enriched with imaginary architectural elements, often in an amusing way. For example, a painted niche contains the portrait bust of the patron, his car keys are painted on the pedestal. Or a painted door, slightly ajar, reveals a

105 *Embellishment of a door panel with wood grain imitation and a violin. (Susanne Müller)*

106 *An unusual and contemporary variation of trompe l'oeil is this investigation into the relationship of architecture and design, on view at the American Arts and Crafts Museum, New York (1988). (Richard Haas)*

7. A Room Without Borders: Painting in Panoramic Format

107 *A prime example of the unity of imaginary and real space: "In front of" the wall are plants and butterflies that cast shadows; "behind" the wall is a view of the ocean. The steps connect receding and advancing elements and make it very difficult to locate the actual surface of the painting. The real but artificial wisteria is part of the design and make it almost impossible to tell fact from fantasy. (Karl Rampp)*

Inside and Outside

"Welcome to a new reality!" This greeting meets all who enter a room with panoramic paintings. The walls have disappeared, inside and outside merge (figure 107). The artistic challenge in the creation of a panoramic picture—independent of the subject—consists in opening up an imaginary space and connecting it to the existing architectural space and all its artistic components. Through the painting we seem to catch glimpses of the outside world beyond the walls and find inside and outside, the real and the painted in a dynamic relationship. No panoramic picture could function as an imaginary world without such interaction. Without a clearly defined *here* we cannot have a *there*; without tangible closeness, there is no visionary distance. The viewer is expected to approach imaginary space and real space with the same certainty. This creative principle was already demonstrated by the ancient Romans as they combined imitative and representative painting in the Second Style. The wall remains a wall but is decorated and enhanced with faux finishes. At the same time, this wall, pierced by apparent door and window openings, seems to dissolve and retreat. The previous chapter shows several further examples of this approach.

An opening is conjured up; we look at a scene that magically seems to lie behind the surface of the wall, and the effect becomes even more vivid if the opening is framed with elements that seem to protrude into actual space. The arcades in figure 108 go even further: the marble half-columns are actually three-dimensional and support the appearance of the receding illusionistic painting. There is a special effect on the right side of the picture. First, the lower part of the right wall was painted with a marble design. This marble then appears as a illusionistic representation on the adjacent wall. The actual wall is reproduced illusionistically and creates depth through layers of arcades.

The painterly repetition of actually existing architectural elements is a highly effective technique for connecting interior and exterior, real and imaginary space in a convincing manner (figure 110). Here too the Romans created archetypes with their colonnaded vestibules that continued the rows of columns into the wall paintings, and the idea is still copied today (figure 109). Illusionistic balustrades are particularly popular around private indoor pools, but they are of limited credibility. Such details might have been commonplace in Italian palazzos and could serve as connecting elements between real and illusionistic space, but in contemporary houses they will more likely be oddities and look out of place. Balustrades appear somewhat more related to the actual interior if they seem to stand on the painted continuation of the actual floor. White balustrades only make sense over a white floor, sandstone tiles call for balustrades painted to look like sandstone. Where a glass door allows a garden view, it might be preferable to forgo the balustrades in favor of stone walls, fences, or pergolas inspired by the actual garden architecture (figure 111). But an actual view into a garden with its seasonal changes can pose problems, and illusions are most convincing when changes of day and night, summer and winter are "neutralized" as much as possible. Artificial plants can be used as elements of the real, painted flowers as elements of the imaginary space to create a connection between both (figures 112 and 113).

Whole disciplines of art and craft meet at this point. Mannerism had angels penetrate the realm of the painting, their stuccoed legs protruding into architectural space. Today we find rocks jutting out from murals, covered in the same colors as the painted rocks on the wall (figure 112). Chapter 10, The Psychology of Deception, discusses such highly effective methods of dissolving traditional boundaries of genres. A panoramic design that achieves its illusionistic purposes through the

109 Free variation on the architectural column theme. Perfect illusion was not the aim, yet the wall seems to open up and extend the view. The painted shadows pick up the floor coloring and create the illusion of continuity and realism. (Theater Itzehoe, architecture and murals: Gottfried Böhm)

108 The painting repeats the motif of actual marble half-columns and the arches they support. In addition, the wall is represented on the wall! A room full of nooks and crannies can be redefined and expanded by the artwork. (Atelier Benad)

110 *This example also integrates existing columns and arches into the design. The wall appears to recede, and there is even enough room for a horse. (Susanne Müller)*

Creating Depth with Color and Line

There are many methods and painterly means of creating the appearance of three-dimensional space on a flat surface. They are used when architecture and landscapes are represented in panoramic murals. Those methods include the judicious use of color and line, light and dark, proportion and composition. Most important of all is linear geometric perspective, which is treated in a chapter of its own because the design of large perspective paintings requires special considerations. The relationship between line and color will be treated independently.

Is there a place for line as constructive element in a painting? This question has been debated hotly since the time of the Renaissance, when the use of perspective was all the rage. Many thought that this new method was exquisitely suited to represent three-dimensional space. One man was of a different opinion—Leonardo da Vinci. He held that a combination of techniques was more effective. He represented distant objects comparatively smaller (see Distant Views: Proportion and Composition below), modified their tonality, and showed their outlines and form less precisely than those of close objects. This method of smudging or "smoking" distant objects was later known as *sfumato.* Colors in the background are shown lighter and bluer than those in the foreground, and these effects alone can suggest depth even without the use of science, geometry, and optics. Many illusionistic paintings of the present day

painted image alone has a certain honesty and integrity. The more the viewers are fooled by stuffed animals or piped-in nature sounds, the greater their insecurity will be. What role are they supposed to play in this setup? Did they happen into a museum's curio cabinet, and are they now part of a didactic exhibit? And what about the other people in the room: are they, perchance, made of wax?

111 *Gravel, palm trees, and white trellises on the outside are all repeated in the mural.*

112 Mountains in the mural blend effortlessly into actual rocks at the foot of the wall. (Karl Rampp)

113 It is almost impossible to tell which plants are natural and which are painted. The wooden floor looks like a footbridge over the painted water. (Rolf Ohst)

attest to the effectiveness of this method. If objects in the background have softer outlines and less intense colors, if they are lighter and more blue, then space is opened up, and that is the most important effect of a panoramic mural. If a painter also defines objects in the foreground with crisp outlines and bright, saturated colors (preferably warm reds with a forward thrust), the impression of open space is practically guaranteed and independent of realistic representation. The means of contrast and sharpness alone can create space and depth. Some motifs are particularly well suited: gracefully painted arches and the delicate tracery of leaves under a blue sky with hazy clouds are ideal subjects to raise a low ceiling. Without precise lines in the foreground, the sky would only be "half as far away" (figures 114 and 115).

Academic landscape paintings of the eighteenth and nineteenth centuries heightened this suggestion of depth by using extremely dark foreground images. The effect can be dramatic, but should be applied cautiously in murals, since it is difficult to reconcile with the surrounding architectural space.

Volume: Light and Dark

Light and dark are central attributes of the physical world. The pictorial representation of volume, the universal property of three-dimensional objects, requires the use of light and dark. The so-called local color, the specific color of the object, is grayed or lightened, which can be done with a glaze of gray or white (figure 117). Another method is to highlight opaque layers of paint with matching shades of gray and occasional opaque spots of white (figure 118). Both methods can be combined to define spatial attributes of objects as well as the shadows they cast on the surrounding area. Volume can be better expressed in architectural objects than with landscape features. In his late works Canaletto practically polarized areas of light and shadow in his paintings and created extremely realistic spaces (figure 116). Today muralists still work according to the same principles. The illusionistic view of a narrow street shown in figure 99 (page 72) owes its realism and drama to the sharp contrasts between areas of light and shadow. Precise shadow lines require virtuosity on the part of the artist and increase the

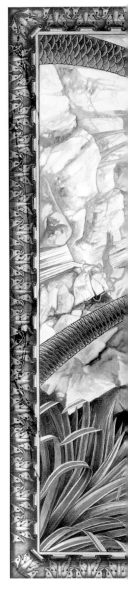

114 *Painted dome. The illusion of space is created through contrasts between warm and cool colors, light and dark, and high and low saturation. (Atelier Fabienne Colin)*

115 *Worm's-eye-view of an exotic scene: Detailed and almost linear elements at the edges of this mural and the dark suspension bridge contrast with the pale blue sky in the distance. (Yannick Guégan)*

illusion that the scene is flooded with sunlight. This approach is daring, since the unequivocal supposition of a single light source—the sun—can easily backfire and disillusion the viewer. Soft, undefined lighting is easier to handle; the focus of the viewers' attention shifts from the purely physical attributes of the landscape to color and general ambiance. The drama of light and dark retreats in favor of soft and lyrical colorations. The romantic clearing in figure 119 shows both approaches: drama and peace of mind in perfect balance.

Sometimes little tricks are indispensable to work with light and shadows. Imagine a viewer who stands in an arcaded walkway and looks out into the landscape with the sun high above it. The arch-

es that frame the view would lie in the shadows, while the features of the landscape would be back-lit, their colors less than brilliant. The painter has the option to make the colors luminous and intense, as if the sun was shining from behind the viewer, and at the same time to paint shadows that contradict such an assumption. Even the arcades themselves can be illuminated miraculously. Light is a necessary prerequisite for seeing; if details on a wall are to be visible, a light source is needed on the side where the viewer stands (see figure 159, page 122). The academic panels that were mentioned earlier have no need for such compromise since they were not conceived as trompe l'oeils and forgo illusionistic relationships with the surrounding space.

117 Design for a mural in watercolor technique. Volume is created through several layers of semi-transparent glazes. (Graham Rust)

118 Strong shades of green and gray were used for this relief; opaque highlights were added for light reflections and stains. (Yannick Guégan)

left:
116 Architectural detail from a painting by Canaletto (1697–1786). The artist combines minute detail with a light-flooded atmosphere. (Louvre, Paris)

119 This romantic image uses light in different ways: dramatic rays illuminate the ruins, trees cast soft shadows, the foliage is full of contrasts and light reflections, and the balustrade in the foreground appears in scattered light. (Rainer Maria Latzke)

120 Depth is created through contrasts, color combinations, and decreasing degrees of sharpness and size in the distance, which leaves us with the question, "How long is that branch really?" (Rolf Ohst)

Distant Views: Proportion and Composition

An easy way to suggest depth is to decrease the size of objects in the distance, as already discussed. Most painters use this method instinctively. Trees, statues, and balustrades in front are large, those in back are small. But mere approximations of size give inaccurate information about the space. To create a convincing illusion it is necessary to follow the laws of perspective, whether intuitively or by a process of careful construction. A branch in figure 120 serves as example. Leaves are smaller the farther away they are from the viewer; the branch itself is foreshortened, but just how long is it? Three yards or fifteen yards—we can only guess. Objects of less biological form are more reliable indicators. Steps, balustrades, columns, lanterns— all have more or less constant dimensions. They serve as guideposts and references in a fictional space. With their help the viewer translates size into distance (figure 121).

Theatrical backdrop paintings do without mathematics. The imaginary space is divided into three layers: foreground, middle ground, and background (figure 124). Painted curtains frequently serve as foreground motif. Drawstrings and tassels gather their folds and cast shadows. This layer defines the front of the space and simultaneously forms a connection to the actual space, which frequently features real curtains. Depth gradations within the layers are possible, but they usually have the character of relief. A vase could be standing at the foot of the curtain, a monkey could be perched there, or a branch could jut out from behind. Such details refine and enliven the layer but remain part of it, independent of the other main layers, such as the balustrade or fence that surrounds a terrace and is shown in considerably smaller size. A layer of plants can be interjected, and the background shows a wide open

landscape, the ocean, distant mountains, or islands. This system of composition is also utilized by a software program that contains landscape elements which can be assembled to make murals in a variety of ways (figure 153, page 115). A logical and amusing application of the principle is shown in figures 122 and 123. Here the image was actually constructed like a stage set, from separately cut-out layers. A final and very important consideration is height, or visibility, of the horizon. We see wide open space if the horizon can be discerned. If this view were obstructed by buildings or vegetation, we would perceive a shallow space. Low horizon lines are popular around pools: they create the impression that the viewer stands on a terrace and would have to descend a few steps to reach street level (figure 125). The same effect would be counterproductive in a jungle scene, where space should be unfathomable, secretive, and full of surprises.

121 *Two spaces: geometrically defined stone patios in the foreground, open vistas in the background. (Rolf Ohst)*

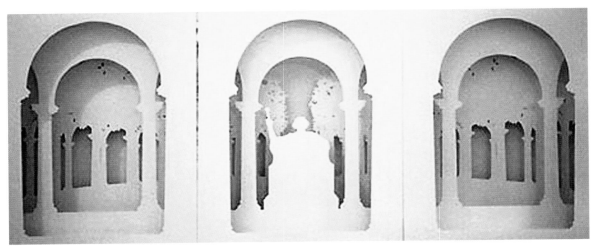

JUSTICE

A high horizon puts the viewer in a low and almost helpless position and invites careful attention to every detail.

Where a painting will only cover part of the wall, special caution applies. Tiles at the base of a bathroom wall, for example, have to be integrated into the design. Such an arrangement usually necessitates a high horizon, and it is best to divide the wall space into several segments, such as windows or arches, through which open space or sky can be seen. Such an arrangement also helps to avoid distortions in small rooms where viewers can stand very close to the painting or see it from radically different angles.

124 The mural in this spa will be viewed up close, from a distance, and from different angles, so depth was created through different layers of pictorial planes rather than through central perspective. (Atelier Benad)

page 92
126 A vast parkscape turns mountainous near the horizon, offers unobstructed views, and lends a generous air and openness to this interior courtyard. The impression of depth is enhanced by a ribbed vault ceiling rendered in perspective, and by pronounced light and dark contrasts. (Atelier Benad)

125 "Over the Rooftops of Grimaud": A pool in a windowless basement acquires an airy vista. (Rainer Maria Latzke)

Conclusion: Opening the Wall—Suggesting Space

Medium	Method	Effect
Real space	• Imitative and representational styles complement each other • Elements that seem to protrude and those that seem to retreat enhance the effect • Elements of architectural and real space are subjects of painting • Transcendence of traditional categories: *Gesamtkunstwerk* to variety of style	• Viewers transfer certainties of real space onto represented objects. Elements of real space can have deceptive aspects
Color	• Aerial perspective: colors lose intensity towards the horizon. They are lighter, hazier (mixed with gray), and slightly bluish • Light-dark contrast: dark and dark gray colors in the foreground frame the motif • Color perspective: "warm" colors in front, "cool" colors behind (e.g., no blue curtains in the foreground; red flowers, not white or purple, for bushes in the foreground)	• A quasi-impressionistic view of the space, creates emotion and participation, but no intellectual challenge. Heightened effect of aerial perspective (a kind of "earth perspective") should be applied sparingly • A quasi-expressionistic view of the space, convincing and expressive. Equally, an appeal to emotion rather than the intellect
Line	• As contour: sharp and precisely defined in front, dissolving and diffused in back (*sfumato*) • As orthogonal lines: lead toward the vanishing point, which represents infinity (see chapter 8)	• Imitates actual seeing process, creates a feeling of space. A sharp focus or diffused treatment differentiates more or less important areas of the painting • Constructs visible appearance according to mathematical principles independent of the original model: suggestive, persuasive, fascinating, rational (more in chapter 8)
Light–dark	• As volume: modeling of objects through gradations of gray • As shadows, particularly cast shadows: shows relationship of objects to each other, makes statements about assumed light sources	• Basic style element to give objects the appearance of reality • Drama, immediacy, realism of a dominant physical world. Shadows as expressive means
Composition	• Proportions: reduction in height and width of various elements in the distance. Distance between them diminishes increasingly • Planes: staggered arrangement. Layers in front partially overlap those in back. Objects on front layers are largest (theatrical backdrop painting) • Position of viewer: general overview (low horizon) or *en face* from short distance (horizon relatively high and hidden behind represented objects)	• Imitates actual seeing process, creates a feeling of space. If size reductions and foreshortenings are done correctly, highly suggestive of geometrical perspective • Theatrical, dramatic aspect of the painting is emphasized. Simple one-point perspective is suggested, e.g., with architectural elements in the foreground • The "all-knowing narrator" observes from a safe distance how others act and suffer (e.g., from an apparently raised terrace). The "ego narrator" is involved in the scene, becomes part of it (e.g., mysterious jungle scenery)

8. Your Point of View: Perspective

127 Ceiling mural in the meeting room of St. Maria Victoria in Ingolstadt. The ceiling is 33 feet (10 m) high; the mural seems to raise it considerably and creates pleasing proportions. The imagery of imposing architecture is best viewed from the entrance; the details at the edges of the mural appear most vivid from a position in the middle of the room. (Cosmos Damian Asam, 1734)

The Art of Seeing Through

Perspective drawings are the daily bread of drafters and interior decorators. But perspective is not just a matter of geometry nor a purely abstract pursuit, even if some handbooks might suggest otherwise. Art historians consider the discovery of central perspective in the late fourteenth century an event of Copernican proportions for the art of painting. Philosophers and theologians debated the spiritual significance of the vanishing point—infinitely far removed, yet visible and representable on a small sheet of paper. In the seventeenth century projective geometry was developed from the study of perspective and is now one of the most fascinating fields of modern mathematics. Computer-animated design systems can now simulate an observer's movement through mind-boggling 3D spaces in real time. The mathematical transformation of three-dimensional space into a two-dimensional surface (or the use of a stereoscopic viewer) brings us to the intersection of two polar entities: the world of art and the senses and the world of abstract science, mathematics, and its objective laws.

There are only a handful of contemporary illusionistic painters who really know their geometry when it comes to constructing perspectives. Much experience is necessary, not just in technical drawing, but also because many special conditions apply for large-scale projects. A painting that is done according to the rules of perspective will have an impact on the viewer that could never be achieved otherwise (figures 128 and 129). But before the special requirements for large formats are discussed, a short explanation of the general principles of perspective is in order.

The Latin word *perspectare* can be translated as "looking" or "seeing through" and implies here that one is looking deep into a space. The art of looking through, *arte prospettiva*, was discovered in the fourteenth century and developed into a geometric method of construction. The essential elements—horizon line and vanishing point—were defined and related to each other. When we speak

above:
128 The painted columns at the end of this corridor in Sabionetta make it appear even longer than it already is and open the view toward infinity. (Vincenzo Scamozzi, 1552–1616)

left:
129 All architectural details for this monumental mural (33 x 20 feet [10 m x 6 m]) were constructed with great precision. We see a sleeping boy in contemporary clothing, and the eighteenth-century scenery might be the vision of his dreams. (Pascal Amblard)

of perspective today, we usually mean central perspective with a main vanishing point near the middle of the picture, as described by Leon Battista Alberti (1404–1474). Of course, there are other forms of perspective, such as parallel or one-point perspective, or axonometric projection. Color and aerial perspective have already been mentioned. Central perspective and similar methods, however, can achieve a special feat. With the help of geometry, a precise image of reality can be constructed, and it is not even necessary to look at that reality and use it as a model. In 1685 Andrea Pozzo designed a complex dome that could not possibly have been copied from anywhere since it would have been statically impossible to construct (figure 130). Nevertheless, it looks so convincing and full

130 Drawing of
Pozzo's dome
from his manual
Perspectiva Pic-
torum et Archi-
tectorum
(1693/98).

*132 Unlike Pozzo's dome this image is oriented
towards a central vanishing point, therefore it is
best viewed from the center of the room.
(Nicola Vigini)*

of realistic details that everyone thinks it illustrates
an existing dome. One of the many paintings
inspired by Pozzo is the ceiling mural in the parish
church of St. Mauritius in Wiesentheid, Germany,
by Giovanni Francesco Marchini (1728/29) (figure
131). Even in this small reproduction the image
has considerable suggestive power. And consider
this: there is no dome in the painted space: Pozzo
created his grand illusion on a vaulted ceiling.
Some contemporary works are reminiscent of his
mastery (figure 132). Sadly, there are few commis-
sions available for domes like Pozzo's today.

131 Ceiling mural in St. Mauritius, Wiesentheid. This stunning fresco is executed on a barrel vault ceiling and combines Pozzo's trompe l'oeil architecture from the nave of St. Ignatius with his trompe l'oeil dome above the choir. (Giovanni Francesco Marchini, 1728/29)

With the Eye of the Spirit

Some images seem to pull the viewer into their depths, and this magnetic force can be explained: The viewer is part of the picture; he or she is contained in the vanishing point and cannot escape the effect. The principle can be explained with the help of a less complicated example: the perspective grid.

The grid in figure 133 is a tool that can be used to represent simple objects with the help of central perspective and does not require complex construction. The lines stand for the invisible optical framework that is a necessary prerequisite for visual perception for all of us. With every glance, we superimpose such a grid over the world around us and make it conform to our perspective view. Figure 134 clarifies this by showing an object in such a grid. In view A the object is relatively far away and we see only its front side; view B brings the viewer closer and somewhat to the side. These illustrate not two different objects but two different views of the same object that result from the viewer's different position relative to the object.

The vanishing point, or point at infinity F, mirrors the position of the viewer's eye at infinity. When the viewer turns and looks to the right, the entire grid shifts towards the right but remains the same! The eye is always inherent in the vanishing point, and all orthogonal lines meet there. The object in the previous example would now have a different position since its edges would no longer be aligned with the grid but viewed at a slant (C). Perspective does not show things as they are, but as they appear to the viewer. Viewer and seeing are constants; the objects of the external world are not.

All this may sound simple enough, but in reality certain limitations apply. First, consider that people have not one but two eyes, and they are constantly in motion. The picture, however, has only one vanishing point, which resides ceremoniously in the middle. Thus, the represented view is only accurate for a one-eyed viewer who stares at the image intently while strapped to a chair and immobilized, which was indeed the position of the early explorers of perspective. Most architectural drawings further show objects in a way that proudly displays the best view with little or no distortion for façades and balustrades, all nicely parallel to the edge of the picture. We assume that the other surfaces are at a right angle to the façade and that they lead into space perspectively, as in views A and B. In fact, nobody ever sees the world in such a simplified and idealistic way. Further exceptions are extreme close-ups or views from extreme distances (consider wide-angle lenses).

Finally, remember that a perspective painting such as a mural has to be viewed from a particular spot if the grid that is inherent in the picture and the one in the eye of the beholder are to overlap. If this is not the case, the image itself becomes a three-dimensional object on view and the viewer will not see the intended illusionistic view. This problem sounds abstract, but is of fundamental importance for mural paintings, and one does not have to be an expert in geometry to understand its implications.

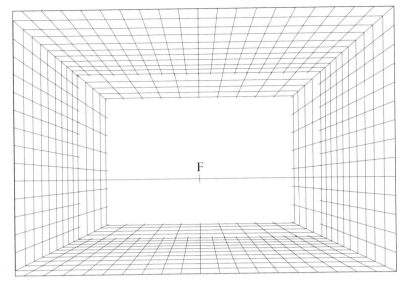

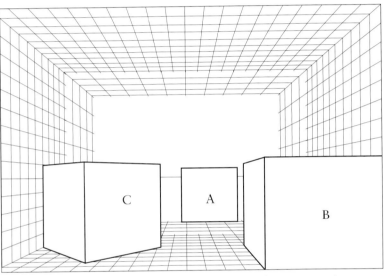

133 *Perspective grids. All lines that meet in the vanishing point at the center of the image are "really" parallel to each other. Since parallels "meet" at a point in infinity, the horizon line, on which the vanishing point is situated, is also infinitely far away. During the fifteenth century, images of God or Christ, the infinite itself, were often positioned in this central area of a painting in recognition of the fact that this vanishing point also represents the seeing eye of the viewer . . .*

134 *. . . The appearance of an object differs depending on the viewer's distance and position.*

137 a, b *The vanishing point of the mural is identical with the one chosen for the observation of the image in its actual position (a). If the observer's viewpoint is raised, the two patterns of perspective contradict each*

135, 136 *The main wall of an indoor swimming pool, en face and from an angle. (Atelier Benad)*

The Geometry of Real Space and Its Continuation in the Picture

Figures 135 and 136 show the same mural. For the first, the camera was held at a right angle towards the picture plane, almost exactly opposite the vanishing point. The painting appears practically undistorted and shows a symmetrical terrace. For the second picture, the camera was moved too far to one side, the wall was photographed from an angle, and the formerly symmetrical view appears slanted. This illustrates the effect that occurs when a viewer moves left or right from the ideal viewing point. But according to the three-dimensionality of space, eye level and distance (depth) also have to be considered. Figures 137a and b show schematic murals from two different points of view. The difference is the eye level. Image a is seen from the correct viewing point; image b is seen from a position that is too high, and the picture looks like a wallpapered photograph that was applied without consideration for the surrounding space and for decoration only.

It is also interesting to consider what happens to the horizon line when a landscape is painted on two or more walls that are at an angle to each other. Figure 138 shows a photo that was taken from an almost ideal viewpoint.

Figures 139a and b illustrate what happens if the eye is above or below the painted horizon line.

When a minimum distance is required for an optimal view of a painting, distortions are particularly obvious for a viewer who stands farther away so orthogonal lines appear incongruous. This effect is most obvious at the transition between painted and real floor tiles, as illustrated in figure 137b, where the floor seems to slant downwards.

If the viewer does not stand in the best viewing position, the result is not just an optical break between real space and picture; logical problems concerning the picture content can also arise. An observer standing to the left of a real object would see the front and the left side of it. If the object is painted accordingly, the viewer should never stand too far to the right of that object, since he or she would then expect to see the right side, which, unfortunately, is not shown in the picture (figure 140). It would be wrong to blame illusionistic painting itself. Its limits are exactly the challenge for every artist, and the rules of the game are to design paintings in such a way that they work best for the most important points of view. Figure 127 (page 94) shows that more than one ideal position is possible, and painters can equally well anticipate viewers who wander about.

other and the landscape seems to slide downwards (b). This phenomenon can also be observed in ceiling murals. When the viewer moves to certain unfavorable viewpoints, the trompe l'oeil architecture can appear to sway.

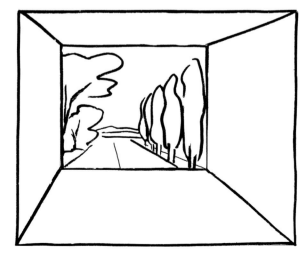

138 *Landscape with animals: The camera lens and the horizon are at almost the same level. There is only a slight angle in the horizon line. (Claus D. Biswanger)*

Mobile Viewers and Picture Design

Viewers walk through foyers, naves, or galleries; they don't just sit motionless in theater seats or relax in deck chairs. There are many ways in which this fact can be exploited artistically, and there are just as many ways to avoid the problem.

▋ During the fifteenth century, when perspective was already known but not yet a topic for illusionistic integration into real space, it was customary to show historical sequences in separate scenes. Each of them was represented in central perspective, and the viewers would move from one to the next, pausing in front of each. The same principle

is still in use today, if in a completely different context: It may be necessary to paint a "neutral" balustrade, one that will not appear illogical whether viewed from left or right, or interfere with another main vanishing point of the picture. This can be achieved by painting each baluster and its base in central perspective or by using cylindrical columns to avoid telltale edges that would give away its orientation.

▋ A similar strategy can be employed in large paintings where orthogonal lines can meet in several vanishing points according to different sections

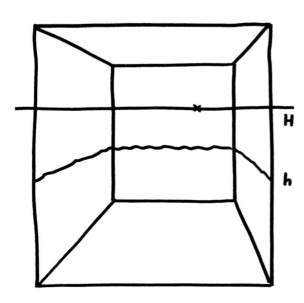

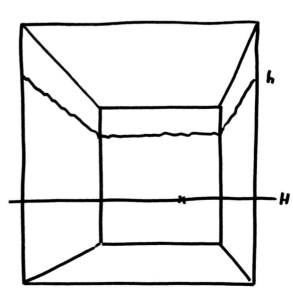

139 *a, b*

In figure a the viewer's eyelevel (H) is higher than the horizon line (h) of the surrounding mural. In figure b the eye level is set considerably below the horizon line of the image. Both scenarios result in a visual break of the painted horizon line.

of the painting. The viewer rarely concentrates on the entire painting at once, and when details are seen up close, "regional perspectives" are admissible or even necessary.

▍A further strategy for avoiding difficulties is the following rule: the deeper the view into space, the fewer orthogonal lines should be visible. Only objects in front should show lines that lead towards the vanishing point. Further back, rambling vines, flowers, or strategically placed statues can obscure problem points and function as perspective fig leaves. In the case of "antique" paintings, the difficult spot can simply be scraped off to imply that the plaster is chipped here.

▍Some painters take advantage of various points of view with great skill. A wall or ceiling mural can coax the viewer into exactly the spots from which the view is most convincing. The position from which figure 127 (page 94) was photographed was probably not chosen by coincidence: it was dictated! Pozzo's St. Ignatius in Rome leads the visitor through the interior of the church through a sequence of viewpoints. In Pompeian villas the best viewpoint frequently marks the most important place in a room: the seat of the master. He alone can see the paintings in all their glory.

▍The play with points of view can also be reversed. The viewer walks through a building and "accidentally" discovers an illusionistic view, a person at a window, for example (figure 141). There she is again, in the next room, exactly as we expect to see her from the new point of view (figure 142). Pure magic!

▍There is yet another way to manipulate a viewer's angle of observation and to influence where exactly the viewer stands: anamorphosis. These images appear completely nonsensical when they are viewed frontally, but make sense from an unusual point of view or when seen with the aid of optical instruments such as cylindrical mirrors. It is up to the viewer to figure out what method of encoding has been used and how the secret image can be revealed. A famous example is an anamorphically distorted skull in Holbein's portrait of two otherwise clearly recognizable diplomats, dated 1533. The bookshelf in figure 102 (page 74), from which a gnome seems to leap, represents a classical trompe l'oeil motif and includes an anamorphosis as well: the little fellow can only be seen three-dimensionally when viewed from an angle. The view from the window with its strange knobs and handles in figure 143 also reveals its true shape only from a side view. One could say that anamorphosis is the opposite of trompe l'oeil, since the latter functions as immediate deception when viewed from the right position, but appears less

140 Every trompe l'oeil painting assumes a particular viewpoint for the viewer. From a different position the image appears illogical. This illustration shows a detail from a painting that is hung approximately at eye level. (Jeanne White)

credible when the viewer's position changes. Anamorphosis, by contrast, freely admits trickery and reveals itself only from extreme vantage points. Still, there are similarities. Figure 144 was photographed from an angle that is inappropriate for its central perspective. The room's main wall on the left is 39 feet (12 m) long and we see it here like someone who has just entered the room. The part of the building that is painted on the left wall should appear grossly distorted in this view, but the opposite is true: it looks completely right, and appears as part of the façade, which is actually quite short. With this optical trick the proportions of the entire room are balanced and improved. Pozzo employed a similar strategy and used anamorphosis in the nave of St. Ignatius. He transferred the grid of a flat cartoon onto a vaulted ceiling with the help of strings and a lamp. The painting represents a distorted version of the original design, but from a certain point of view the distortion cannot be perceived and the columns seem to rise straight into heaven. A prime example of an

141, 142 Nude at a window. These paintings were made for two different rooms in the same house. In the entrance hall (142) the visitor marvels at the brilliant trompe l'oeil while recognizing it as such, and is all the more surprised to find the second image later (141). (Ron Francis)

anamorphosis that also has the character of a trompe l'oeil is shown in figures 145 and 146. Only one point of view reveals an "ordered" spiral (figure 145). Anyone who enters through the main door is faced with a centrifugally distorted image of forms that cannot be identified as any particular geometric object (figure 146). This image changes as the viewer moves through the hallway. One has to turn back at the end of the hallway to see the motif that inspired the painting: an elliptical staircase that actually exists in another part of the building.

144 Mural around an indoor swimming pool. The roofline of the house on the left wall is a continuation of the right wall. (Atelier Benad)

143 Anamor-phism: This im-age should be viewed at an angle from the right. (Ron Francis)

Conclusion: Best Uses of Perspective

1. Perspective can create a convincing impression of depth if the geometry of the actual space seems to continue into the painting. It is the best link between imaginary and architectural space.

2. Perspective representations define a particular point from which an observer should look at the painting. The viewer and the act of seeing are part of the painting. Artists like Escher fool the viewer when they show "impossible" figures in perspective, and we see that this perspective does not just make an imaginary space accessible to the mind, as we see in layered stage sets or backdrops or in aerial perspective, but the viewer is surprised by an experience and can't believe his or her own eyes.

3. The greatest challenge for illusionistic paintings is to anticipate the movements of the viewers. This problem can be dealt with in the following ways:

▌ Orthogonal lines are only shown on elements in the foreground. For those farther back, set-painting techniques and other methods to suggest depth are applied.

▌ For large paintings that will also be viewed close up, several relatively independent perspectives can be applied, or the vanishing point can be moved along a vertical or horizontal axis until the ques-

tionable sections at the edge of large paintings simply disappear.

▌ Unacceptable violations of logic can be avoided by using architectural elements in cylindrical form, by covering problem spots with leaves, or by simply physically eliminating that section of the painting.

▌ A horizon line that spans across several walls needs special attention. Architectural elements or plants in the corners can camouflage the bend that will inevitably appear from certain viewpoints.

4. A change of position can be used as an expressive element:

▌ The painting leads the viewer to particular positions, creates a choreography of movement, and assigns importance to certain spots of the actual space.

▌ One motif can be represented in several discrete views, each with a perspective appropriate to the view point.

▌ Anamorphoses are fascinating amusements. They can also be used to conceal problems in the proportions of a room.

▌ Pictures that play with a variety of viewpoints can also invite the viewer to explore his or her own powers of perception.

145, 146 *A combination of wall and ceiling paintings
with floor mosaic. The pictures show two totally surprising and unpredictable views from the ends of the same
hallway that connects old and new parts of a building.
The effect is created through an elliptical spiral and seems
to remind us that there is no universally valid point of
view. (Haubitz + Zoche)*

9. Materials and Techniques

What techniques and what materials should the painter chose? What requirements must a ground serve, and how durable will it be?

The Fresco Technique

Modern murals are rarely true frescoes in the classical sense (figure 148). The word *fresco* comes from the Italian *dipingere a fresco*, which can be translated as "painting on the fresh (wall)." Traditionally, one paints onto fresh plaster with pigments that are dissolved in water or in limewater. When it dries, calcium carbonate forms and encloses the pigment particles in its structure. The pigment is now not just adhered to the wall but calcified in it.

The traditional elements of a fresco are:
▌ A first rough undercoating of hydrated lime, rough sand, and fine pebbles on a well-dampened wall to even out irregularities in the surface. This layer also acts as a buffer against humidity.
▌ An undercoating of a mixture of hydrated lime and sand. Charcoal outlines of the design can be drawn on this layer.
▌ A painting coat of hydrated lime and fine sand. Paint must be applied to this layer before it dries and forms a crust. Therefore, the painter only applies as much of this coat as can be covered with paint in one day. The outline of the *giornata* (the day's work) traces a suitably large segment of the design. Fresh mortar, or *intonaco*, is applied the next day for subsequent sections.

Only alkali-resistant pigments can be used for this kind of painting, which results in the typical fresco palette. Experience is essential, from the preparation of the mortar to the swift completion of the *giornata* before the mortar dries. Paints look considerably darker when they are freshly applied and still wet, and it is hard to predict the exact shade of the completely dried paint. Every brushstroke has to be right since corrections are possible only by chiseling or cutting away an entire section of mortar.

Today walls are usually not prepared meticulously by hand, but mechanically. Matte highlights and the "authentic charm" of the fresco can be achieved

147 Mineral colors were used when the ceiling of the middle pavilion was newly decorated in the Grossen Orangerie, Charlottenburg Palace, in Berlin. (Peter Schubert)

149 *The curtain of the Odéon Theater in Paris was recreated after historical models. The pigments were mixed with traditional rabbit glue because other binders could cause reflections from the spotlights. (Jean Claude Bobin)*

148 *Tiepolo's murals in the castle of Würzburg were done in true fresco technique. This view shows the grand staircase.*

through shortcuts. Public building projects, for instance, often utilize a technique in which a wash of plaster is applied over an already set ground shortly before painting *a fresco*. Ready-made grounds are also available commercially.

Mineral Colors

The use of mineral colors produces an effect similar to that of the fresco technique on wet plaster (figure 147). In contrast, the secco technique (*secco*—Italian for "dry") involves painting on dry plaster (an exception is lime-casein paints). Mineral colors have been used with great success since the second half of the nineteenth century. Paintings created with them are even more durable than frescoes and show greater resistance to the effects of air pollution. Therefore, mineral colors are often chosen for outdoor murals, less frequently for indoor work. Pigments have to be alkali-resistant, and the palette is similar to the one available for frescoes. Potassium silica, a derivative of silicic acid, is used as binder;

the paint adheres to the wall with the help of a diluted potassium silica fixative spray that causes a reaction of the pigments with the prepared ground and results in permanent fusion. Modern one-component dispersion silica colors contain pigments, binders, and additives in a ready-to-use mix. Additional fixatives become unnecessary. While acrylic, oil, and tempera paints always form a film, the mineral colors do not seal the pores of the ground, which remains permeable to humidity.

Casein Paints

Casein paints, also known as milk, or farmers', paints, are the only possible choice of glue-based paint for murals, where durability is of the essence. Their main advantage is that they can be applied directly onto untreated plaster, even if has not dried completely. The resulting paintings are highly durable and the technique is often used in restoration projects. Here too the palette consists of alkali-resistant pigments (figure 149).

Tempera Paints

These paints are based on watery or oily emulsions, for example, casein tempera or egg tempera. For murals, only paints with a high water content can be used, and the most frequent application of tempera today is the restoration of existing tempera paintings (such as the picture on the title page of this book).

Acrylic Paints

The majority of contemporary illusionistic paintings in interior spaces are done with acrylic paints (figure 150). Since the first acrylics for artists were developed in the 1960s, acrylics have replaced lacquers and other products and gained primacy not just in the fine arts but also in the building industry. The advantages of acrylic resin-based paints are:

▌ They are water soluble, and can be thinned with water.

▌ They are low in odors and emissions.

▌ They have a (limited) permeability for moisture.

▌ A large palette of lightfast colors is available.

▌ The paints are easy to work with and are suitable for techniques from airbrushing to impasto. Even thin glazes can be achieved.

▌ Acrylic paintings can be extremely durable, especially when they are sealed with clear varnish, which can be matte, gloss, or any degree of semi-gloss. Varnish protects a surface not only from mechanical stress, but also from ultraviolet radiation. For paintings that must withstand particularly rough treatments, such as steam cleaning, a two-component acrylic varnish should be used.

However, acrylics have these drawbacks:

▌ Acrylics cannot be applied as finely as oils and have less transparency and depth.

▌ Acrylics dry quickly, but the process can be prolonged by adding thickeners, retardants, or glazes. These additives reduce the durability of the paint layer because they tend to cause swelling under humid conditions. A higher content of binder can counteract this effect to a certain extent.

▌ The artist has to anticipate that acrylic paints will darken slightly during the drying process, and adjust tonality accordingly. With some experience, this is usually not a problem.

▌ If the humidity is above 85 percent and temperatures are low, acrylic paints will not dry completely. It is therefore important to control the climate of the work space accordingly while work is in progress.

The pigments in acrylics have a high degree of fineness, and acrylics are usually applied to walls

150 Acrylic paints are relatively easy to work with and have many excellent properties. Many muralists prefer to work in this medium. (Pascal Amblard)

that are smooth as paper. The masonry is prepared with a fine plaster–acrylic mix. A second ground is added to regulate humidity; next comes a synthetic white under-paint layer that further reduces the absorption of liquids and acts a brilliant reflector for the subsequent painting. Most artists request only a smooth wall from the builder and prepare all other necessary layers personally. The builder's preparations are similar to those that would be necessary for a fine fabric wallpaper, a useful formulation in the search for a contractor. If cracks must be anticipated, it is advisable to stabilize the entire surface by gluing on a layer of fabric.

Artists are well advised to examine the wall carefully under different light conditions, including those that will prevail after completion of the mural. Some irregularities of the ground can only be detected under certain conditions. While the work is in progress, the artist may prefer even illumination, daylight or diffused floodlights, but the final lighting may come from spotlights or downlights.

Where ecological building materials and a high permeability for moisture are preferred, acrylic paints should be used sparingly. Exceptions are indoor pools that are surrounded by vapor barrier walls.

Tints and Emulsion Paints

These paints are similar to artist's-grade acrylics and are available to artists in special hues, quality, and packaging sizes. They can be used as glazes but can appear coarser, denser, and even duller than artist's-grade paints; however, some artists who have experience with these paints prefer them to acrylics.

Oil Paints

Trompe l'oeil paintings are executed in artist's oils when a painting "in the style of the old masters" or an elaborate and perfect imitation of wood or marble is desired. But it is easier to paint with oils on panels or canvas that will later be mounted or glued to the wall. Murals are almost never executed in oils.

One reason is that the ground must be almost completely sealed, or at least elaborately primed, to keep it from absorbing the paint. Irregular absorption properties cause differences in color intensity. Since varnished oil paintings are practically impermeable to moisture, all physical aspects of wall construction have to be considered carefully.

A second reason not to use oils is their long drying time, which can be an advantage but necessitates hours or even days of waiting before a new layer of paint can be applied (unless egg tempera was used as under-painting or the entire picture is finished all at once). Slow-drying paint is also a magnet for dust, which is a particular problem if other construction work is being done in the vicinity of the painting in progress.

Consider also that all oil paints and particularly all varnishes are subject to yellowing. The gloss itself can be a problem. Even when a matte agent is added to the final varnish, it is impossible to achieve a completely matte surface with oil paints. Gloss can add to the expressive character of colors, but oil paints should be avoided where light effects and reflections would counteract the desired illusionistic effects.

Still, many fine artists prefer oils for their unrivalled depth and subtle gradations. Some artists who are experienced in the use of oils resist a change to acrylics because oil paints look exactly the same wet or dry. The paint industry is making great efforts to create acrylics with all the positive properties of oil but has not yet succeeded.

Besides the traditional materials and techniques, the following methods are also available to artists today:

Airbrushing

Airbrushing is a modern application with a range of expression that is rarely associated with murals, but it can be highly effective for contemporary and theatrical motifs such as "New York by night" or "Sunset over a South Sea beach." Some artists use the airbrush to supplement acrylic painting, particularly for large areas of sky or for the fuzzy shadows of objects in the background that have already been painted by hand. Artists who value their personal handwriting and expressive style might find airbrushed images cool and anonymous.

Portable Grounds

It can be very helpful to paint certain parts of a work in acrylic, oil, or tempera not on the wall itself but in the studio.

Not all parts of a work in acrylics, oil, or tempera have to be painted directly onto the wall. It can be very convenient to use other supports, work in the studio, and install the painting in the intended location later (figure 151). Possible supports are paper, canvas, or board. Here are some of the advantages:

■ The artist does not have to work exclusively on location, which can save time and travel expenses.

■ The artist can work in the studio without disturbance, has better control over the time schedule, and is able to work on the painting before the walls are completed.

■ Work in difficult locations such as at a great height or on the ceiling is minimized (figures 152 and 154).

■ The duration of work time at the site is shortened. This is particularly an advantage for commercial projects, since the space can be utilized earlier.

It is common practice to paint larger areas such as water, skies, and landscapes on location and directly on the wall, but to finish details like delicate architecture, statuary, animals, and plants in the studio. Later these are applied to the mural with adhesive or spatulas.

A good choice for supports is high-quality paper that will not warp when adhesive is applied and that can withstand subsequent varnishing. Fabrics for supports should be made of polyester, since cotton and linen will shrink in humid conditions. The thread count should be high, so the structure of the weave is as unnoticeable as possible, but at a height or on ceilings even rough weaves cannot be detected.

Vinyl sheets can also be used as grounds, particularly for oil paints. The plastic material is nonabsorptive, completely smooth, and practically indestructible. Paints "stand" on the smooth surface and can be manipulated for a long time. It is best to tailor the size of the sheets to the dimensions of the panels or coffers that have to be decorated and to avoid joints.

On wall sections where joints can be hidden, formats of up to 54 square feet (5m²) can be painted on lightweight panels such as plywood or particle board. The panels are then mounted and can be removed and reused, in a different location if necessary. This material is very popular in the food business and in private homes because the investment for the painting is not tied to the actual locale, which may only be leased.

151 A canvas was painted in the studio and glued to the wall on location. (Atelier Benad)

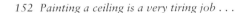

152 Painting a ceiling is a very tiring job . . .

Industrial Production Methods

Besides photographic wallpapers, reproductions of trompe l'oeil paintings on synthetic panels or plywood are available and can be mounted easily. If necessary, an air-circulation system can be installed behind the panels. Numbered editions that have been designed by artists expressly for the purpose are popular. Computer technology has made a variety of options available. Software offers a variety of landscapes and sky and ocean views as well as details such as vases, urns, balustrades, and plants. Designs can be created on a PC and fitted to the exact measurements of the walls. They are then emailed to a production studio, transferred onto large canvasses with specially-developed techniques, and finally glued in place on location (figure 153).

153 A mural is composed on a computer and transferred onto canvas. (Fresco Master)

154 . . . which sometimes cannot be avoided. Here a balustrade was added to an existing mural to integrate with the existing architecture. It is hard to believe that figures 152 and 154 show the same balustrade. It all depends on one's point of view! (Jean-Claude Bobin)

10. The Psychology of Deception

155 *These courtiers are not even among the main characters that grace Tiepolo's Emperor Hall in the castle in Würzburg, but they could not be more lively and expressive.*

Illusionistic Painting: Art and Life

Illusions cannot be painted. Paintings are part of our physical surroundings; they really exist, but illusions are fantasy, fiction, or wishful thinking. They are part of our interior psychological world, originating in the consciousness as "private affairs" when perceptions are misinterpreted. It is the objective of illusionistic painting that observers should misinterpret the signals from their eyes and consider the painted object real. The term *trompe l'oeil*—fooling the eye—is actually wrong, since it is not the eye that is fooled, but the mind that interprets the image.

The paradox is that illusionistic painting is interpreted "correctly" only when it is misinterpreted, in other words; when we fall for the deception. It is even part of the plan that the viewer will eventually see through that deception and enjoy it anyway because of its beauty. The dividing line between reality and illusion can be drawn in intellectual analysis, but not during the moment of the actual experience. It is pleasurable to be deceived in this way—charmed, enchanted, whisked away to other realms, and one admires the artist who performs such magic.

The oscillating relationship between image and viewer is characteristic of illusionistic painting, but it is not limited to this medium. Theater is another example. Eeveryone knows that the action on stage is not real, yet viewers treat it as such and become emotionally involved with the characters. Stage architecture signifies various levels of reality. Classical illusionistic stages are framed by curtains and define a specific place for the action of the play. The proscenium defines another reality: actors step out of the framed reality of their play and speak directly to the audience. A simple television set makes do without such architectural language, yet countless viewers treat the daily soaps as real-life episodes, and try to find out the phone numbers of the characters, not those of the actors.

Frames are essential elements in the relationship of art and everyday life, and not just the frames around pictures, stages, or television screens. Any

157 *An idealized landscape in a bathroom. The mirror behind the sinks reflects the painting on the opposite wall. Only half of the marble vase is painted; the mirror completes it. (Atelier Benad)*

object recognizable as artwork has a frame that separates it from everyday life and is thus at a so-called aesthetic distance from the viewer. Illusionistic painting bridges exactly that distance. Viewers cannot tell if they are admiring a work of art or looking at things as they are; they are in a state of aesthetic limbo. Artists starting in the twentieth century have questioned art itself with their work and dissolve the boundaries between art and life. These are obvious parallels to illusionistic painting with one important difference: Contemporary illusionistic paintings can still be interpreted like "old-fashioned" paintings and have an autonomy that modern art often lacks, since modernity often implies interactivity, an incompleteness, and a need for a visitor who touches the work or interacts with it in some way.

Illusionistic art also contains this aspect of the avant-garde: it invites participation. The theater of the baroque, to mention an example from the past, presented a clear example of this. The events on stage were only one part of the evening's performance; the audience, which often considered plot and actors as something of a side show, set itself into the scene during and after the play and thus provided the other half of the evening's entertainment. Art and play—life should be like this, and courtly ceremony is a form of theater, too. Whether this fact satisfies the saying "everyone is an artist" remains unanswered. Still, similarities to modern show business are striking. One can join the clapping audience of a television show and appear on the neighbors' television screens, or, better yet, get the part of a lifetime in a television reality show. In our current societal and social settings it is exactly the "old-fashioned" realism that illusionistic painting is often accused of that constitutes its characteristic strength. The realism of the representation becomes the means to transcend aesthetic boundaries and dissolve the division between art and life. The true substance of an illusionistic painting is not to be found on the wall, but in the living reality that surrounds it and is in constant interaction with it.

Illusionistic painting plays with viewers, with their perceptions, and their traditional role. It is not associated with any particular style or time period, and it should be easy enough to refute any accusations that it is mere decoration or superficial embellishment.

The Latin word *ludus* means game, *illudere* means to play, to conjure up. The positive aspects are exemplified in figures 156 and 158. A slightly more sinister dimension of illusionistic painting is possible where willful deception is at work.

Murals and Photographic Wallpaper

The mysterious relationship between art and reality occupies the mind of many artists, and libraries could be filled with texts on the subject. Here are some thoughts on the relationship between illusionistic painting and photographic wallpaper.

We all live in our own world and have a limited horizon. The "real" world is created by our thoughts, images, feelings, and actions. For a child, the moon might be a disk within her grasp; for a hunter the moon illuminates the forest at night; for a pair of lovers it is an accessory to a romantic evening; an astronomer searches it for distant craters; to a physicist it is a chunk of matter in orbit. Therefore, it is obviously wrong to say that a photograph shows nature as it really is, and it is easy to understand why an enlarged snapshot glued to the wall does not automatically give the viewer the impression of being whisked away to the depicted location, maybe a beach with swaying palm trees. The very elements that that make such a process possible are usually missing in a photograph.

The object needs to be "optimized." The artist depicts the beach in a way that lets the viewer share in the atmosphere of the actual place. This has nothing to do with realism or naturalism;

158 A restaurant on a cruise ship with a "view" of an underwater world. (Richard Haas)

rather, it is an idealized representation according to particular, often emotional aspects. Examples from nature are chosen for the picture to convey exactly the right feeling. Sometimes the ideal motif might be a Roman villa that does not even exist any longer, and therefore could not be photographed. Decay, cracks, and patina can be included in the design to reinforce the suggestion of age.

Beyond idealization, the artist always has to remember that the overall composition is an original creation for a specific project, and not a natural phenomenon. The creator of illusionistic paintings does not paint the world as it is, but as the client expects it to be (figures 157, 159). The same is true for imitations of materials. Only the most characteristic properties of oak panels or the delicate diagonal veins of Carrara marble are represented; the more average examples are less interesting. One exception is the trompe l'oeil panel, which does not idealize. On the contrary, it presents everyday objects in a highly specific context, which makes them seem important and all the more noteworthy.

Imitation, Representation, or Creation?

Imitating nature, the ideal of classical art, is once again the aim of many artists. The artwork is meant to be as close to the appearance in nature as possible. Copying and imitation is at a new high. It is not enough to paint a picturesque place such as San Marco in Venice, but sometimes the slice of reality is reconstructed in three dimensions, so that the Grand Canal may flow through Las Vegas and the Swiss Alps, in the form of artificial rocks, reaching as far as fitness rooms in Japanese spas. Other tools are lighting effects to simulate day or night, sound systems, or video installations, all to perfect the illusion. But do they really succeed? In contrast to classical illusionistic paintings, many of these transplanted installations appear so unlikely in their new surrounding that their viewers or inhabitants would need a very high level of motivation to go along with the deception. The viewer feels not so much "in Venice" or "in the Alps" as like an actor in a movie or a play with the corresponding title. The aesthetic pleasure of a back-and-forth between illusion and recognition is lost in a three-dimensional theme park that can be touched and walked through and provides stimulation for all the senses at once.

There is an entirely different approach towards a painting. It can be seen as representation of reality rather than a copy, and this representation has a dynamic connection to the original. It is this attitude that makes the veneration of icons possible: what is worshiped is not the picture itself but the saint that appears in it. The image is a beacon for the consciousness of the viewer, but not every painting of a saint is necessarily a venerable icon. Strict rules apply and have historical foundations. It was believed that the original models for icons were not made by human hands but were direct emanations of the represented person. In 787 the Second Council of Nicea was called to settle the question of iconoclasm and defined the connection between image and reality in theological terms. What may seem like an ancient and irrelevant religious discussion actually deals with issues that are still of importance today. Why should it not be possible that the painted image of a thing, a person, or an event could be inspired by the original? A picture might direct the viewers' attention

159 *View through an arch flanked by columns. The point of view is slightly raised and shows an idyllic Tuscan landscape. (Atelier Benad)*

existing image in the viewer's mind. The artist's "small creation" has similar visual effects on the viewer as the "big creation." To look at a well-painted palm tree and not realize that a palm tree is being represented is as much an impossibility as to follow these instructions: "Imagine that you are intensely not thinking of the ocean and a beautiful beach!" Well-painted does not necessarily mean painted in great detail. For an image that is meant to be seen from a 60-foot (20 m) distance fewer details will be needed than for one that will be seen up close. The process of identifying a painterly arrangement of color and form as a particular object is already considered illusionistic deception by many philosophers. They consider representational art shadowy images, fleeting impressions that have nothing to do with reality itself.

But illusionistic painting is much more than just representational, and the deception that it produces is much stronger. The viewer believes that the image before his eyes is not a painting of something, but the thing itself. Illusionistic painting conceals itself to seduce the viewer into believing that the image is real, to assign reality status to it. If the maneuver is to be successful the artist has to appeal to three levels:

▌ Intellect: The represented objects are "probable." One believes that they could exist. Even if it is rather unlikely that one could find a stretch of Caribbean oceanfront in Chicago, for example, the painted verandah fits in and acts as a "reality bridge."

▌ Emotion: The painting is brimming with sensuous details. A profusion of objects and sensations

toward inner qualities of reality that they would otherwise ignore. This function is described in chapter 2 (Sources of Strength) and can also apply to representational paintings.

At different ends of the spectrum are imitation that focuses only on surface appearance and the creation of a work of art that orients itself around Plato's Theory of Ideas (but not his approach to art). Between those extremes lies a wide range of different views and manifestoes, even among illusionistic painters. But all have this in common: to the best of their ability they recreate a part of the world, or should we say they create a part of the world, and they entrust it to the viewers' perception. It is this personal awareness and interpretation that hold the key to illusionistic painting.

From Perception to Participation

It is a tricky question, whether it is painters who create the image or if their skillful arrangement of paint and form become images only in the eye of the beholder. After all, short horizontal brush-strokes, even if they are slightly wavy and in shades of blue, do not necessarily signify Ocean. The important thing is that an association is created between the image at hand and an already

160, 161 Many indoor swimming pools are located in windowless rooms, and can be transformed completely through paintings and light effects. If these imaginary worlds match the tastes and needs of the users, if they

create feelings of spaciousness and relaxation, if they satisfy the viewers' desire for classical, naturalistic, or other themes, then trompe l'oeil paintings have done their job well. (Below: Karl Rampp; above right: Rolf Ohst)

is presented, and everything is offered with skill, grace, and extravagant generosity. Any necessary abstractions or stylizations only serve to heighten these effects.

▌ Motivation: Illusionist paintings invite viewers to get involved. The illusion of space is easiest to maintain; once viewers succumb to it their ability to perceive and decode images makes them part of a (presumed) new reality. A contemplative pleasure becomes a challenge to act, since three-dimensionality can be explored physically, one can walk through it, and touch it, and not just look at it. At this point begins the actual confrontation with the work: viewers step forward and back again, try out different viewing angles, touch the wall and try to figure out it if it is painted or "real." Eventually the deception is revealed, but the viewers are already participants in the game. Here, at the very latest, they recognize that they have the option to play a bigger role than just to verify their own interpretations. We are back at the topic of *ludus*, the game. The Caribbean in Chicago will work, but only if the viewers play along (figures 160, 161) .

162 *Life-size portraits of the Duke of Mantua's horses in the Palazzo del Té.*
To appreciate this unusual composition fully it should be viewed on location.
(Giulio Romano, 1494–1546)

The Secret Presence of the Artist

Technical reproductions of artwork are made in high quality these days, but the original will always differ from the copy because of its history and radiance, which cannot be duplicated (see figure 162). The presence of the artist remains alive in every one of his or her works: "Leonardo made this brush stroke with his own hand." But the liveliness and immediacy of the original artwork comes not only from its historical authenticity, which, as we know, is in question at times—that brushstroke could have been made by one of Leonardo's apprentices. It also comes from the language of the medium itself. Where a brushstroke turns into a wave right in front of the viewer's eyes

because of that viewer's powers of interpretation, there is an immediacy that cannot be reproduced on the pages of any book. Strange, but true. But if it is not just any wave, but an especially expressive or moving one, then the viewer might feel connected to the artist who has captured all those emotions in the painting, leaving it to the viewer to rediscover them. The image is truly animated by the touch of the artist. The maturity and experience of the artist have great impact on the quality of the work. Huge decorative images can be quite bland if they were produced by an unknown hired hand or in assembly-line fashion, while how imposing is even a minor figure by Tiepolo (figure 155).

Bibliography

For those who need further information on specific subjects, the following annotated list offers a choice of recommended works which the authors consulted in preparation for this work in addition to their own professional experience and exchanges with colleagues. General art history books and artists' monographs are not listed.

Murals, Antique to Modern

Varone, Antonio, and Erich Lessing. *Pompeii*. Paris: Finest S.A./Editions Pierre Terrail, 1996.
Easy to read overview, describes artistic developments in the mirror of political and societal events. Exquisite photographs of architecture, murals, and decorative objects enliven the work. Extensive bibliography.

Rozenberg, Silvia. *Enchanted Landscapes. Wall Paintings from the Roman Era*. London: Thames and Hudson, 1994.
From the many works on Roman-Pompeian murals this exhibition catalog was chosen because its attractive detail photographs are of particular interest to designers. Emphasis is on the Fourth Style.

Phillipot, Paul. *Die Wandmalerei, Entwicklung Technik Eigenart* (Murals: history, technique, and properties). Vienna, Munich: Verlag Anton Schrell & Co, 1972.
A stimulating overview of mural history. Cultural, historical, and stylistic connections are discussed, detailed information on materials and techniques is given.

Milman, Miriam. *Trompe-L'Oeil Painted Architecture*. New York: Rizzoli, 1986.
Thoroughly researched, fascinating illustrations, and a historically as well as psychologically interesting text makes this book an indispensable standard work of trompe l'oeil architecture murals.

Wrigley, Lynette. *Trompe L'Oeil: Murals and Decorative Wall Painting*. London: New Holland (Publishers) Ltd, 1997.

Cass, Caroline. *Grand Illusions. Contemporary Interior Murals*. London: Phaidon, 1988.
Both books primarily represent decorative and illusionistic works of contemporary British and American artists. The focus is on murals; panels are not included.

Trompe L'Oeil Painting

Battersby, Martin. *Trompe-L'Oeil. The Eye Deceived*. New York: St. Martins, 1974.

Guégan, Yannick. *Trompe L'Oeil Panels and Panoramas*. New York: W. W. Norton, 2003.

Milman, Miriam. *Trompe L'Oeil Painting: The Illusions of Reality*. New York: Rizzoli, 1987.

Mauriès, Patrick (editor). *Trompe l'oeil. Das getäuschte Auge* (The deceived eye). Cologne: DuMont, 1998.

Monneret, Jean. *Le triomphe du trompe-l'œil: Histoire du trompe-l'œil dans la peinture occidentale du Ve siècle avant J.-C. à nos jours.* (The triumph of trompe l'oeil: history of trompe l'oeil in Western painting from the 5th century B.C. to the present). Paris: Menges, 1993.

The four above titles are scientifically oriented and represent the art of trompe l'oeil from antiquity to the present in accessible style; they offer rich illustrations and extensive bibliographies. Illustrations of 20th century works focus on panel paintings.

Monestier, Martin. *Le Trompe-l'oeil contemporain. Les maîtres du réalisme* (Contemporary trompe l'oeil: the masters of realism). Paris: Menges, 1993.
This lavishly illustrated work gives an overview of the work of contemporary trompe l'oeil artists but does not include murals.

Rodríguez, Ramón de Jesús. *Neue Illusionsmalerei. Entwurf, Technik, Gestaltung* (New trompe l'oeil: planning, technique, design). Munich: Callwey, 2000.
This work is a German translation from the Spanish and an example for the free interpretation of the term "illusionistic painting." The decorative examples don't always attest to great technical skills but show how the integration of paintings and construction jobs can be easy and joyful.

Nouvel-Kammerer, Odile. *French Scenic Wallpaper 1795–1865*. Paris: Flammarion (Musée des Arts décoratifs), 2000.
Luxury edition with reproductions of French panoramic wallpapers in trompe l'oeil style. The artful designs in this collection can be used by painters as models for their own illusionistic work, or, put more elegantly: it is a source of inspiration.

ILLUSIONISTIC PAINTING IN ART THEORY AND ART HISTORY

Gombrich, Ernst H. *Art and Illusion: A Study in the Psychology of Pictorial Representation.* London: Phaidon, 1998.
Classic inquiry into the problem of representation in the art of painting in the context of art history.

Schütz, Heinz. *Barocktheater und Illusion* (Baroque theater and illusion). Europ. Hochschulschriften XXX: 15. Frankfurt am Main: Verlag Peter Lang, 1984.
A historic excursion into the "time of illusionistic phenomena" that considered the whole world a stage. Astute analyses and discourses on psychology and aesthetics of baroque theater and aesthetic illusionism.

Illusionen. Das Spiel mit dem Schein (Illusions. The game of appearances), Vienna: Catalog of the 198th special exhibit of the Historical Museum of Vienna, 1995/1996.
From mechanical viewers to painted illusionism and imaginary worlds, a wide selection of virtual reality's precursors during the 19th century.

GRISAILLE

Krieger, Michaela. *Grisaille als Metapher. Zum Entstehen der Peinture en Camaïeu im frühen 14. Jahrhundert* (Grisaille as metaphor: development of monochrome painting in the early 14th century). Vienna: Verlag Adolf Holzhausens Nachfolger Ges. M.b.H., 1995

Grams-Thieme, Marion. *Lebendige Steine. Studien zur niederlaendischen Grisaille Malerei des 15. und frühen 16. Jahrhunderts* (Living stones. Studies of Netherlandish grisaille of the 15th and early 16th centuries). (Dissertation). Cologne: Böhlau Verlag, 1988.
The two above titles are scientific studies in the areas of art history and philosophy.

FAUX SURFACES

Finkelstein, Pierre. *The Art of Faux: The Complete Sourcebook of Decorative Painted Finishes.* New York: Watson-Guptill, 1997.
Fascinating handbook by a leading specialist, step-by-step instructions for the production of faux surfaces. Masterful projects, brilliant photos.

Guégan, Yannick, and Roger Le Puil. *The Handbook of Painted Decoration: The Tools, Materials, and Step-by-Step Techniques of Trompe L'Oeil Painting.* New York: W. W. Norton & Company, 1996.
This volume of almost 500 pages contains the English translation of six French originals. Topics are wood and marble imitations, patinas, friezes and ornaments, draperies, and other decorative techniques. An inexhaustible wealth of inspiration for painters.

Trouvé, Gérard. *Peinture Decorative: Marbres et bois en trompe-l'oeil, patines et ornementations* (Decorative painting: marble and wood in trompe l'oeil, patinas, and ornamentation). Paris: Pierrefon, 1993.
Luxury edition in large format. Whole page illustrations of marble and wood imitations in excellent reproductions, plus smaller pictures and examples. Sparing text.

PERSPECTIVE

Panovsky, Erwin. *Perspective as Symbolic Form.* Zone Books, 1997.
Panovsky's brilliant essay from 1924/25 will still be enjoyed by anyone who is interested not just in applications for perspective but also in its liberal-arts context.

Abels, Joscijka Gabriele. *Erkenntnis der Bilder. Die Perspektive in der Kunst der Renaissance* (Understanding pictures: Perspective in the art of the renaissance). Frankfurt am Main, New York: Campus Verlag, 1985.
The author shows basic psychological and aesthetic pursuits in specific works by artists from Brunelleschi to Leonardo.

Vredeman de Vries, Jan. *Perspective.* (Reprint of 1604 edition.) New York: Dover Publications, 1968.

Numerous modern handbooks teach the construction methods of perspective, but we are not aware of any that treat the problems of large-scale murals comprehensively. The two above reprints of historical manuals are particularly recommended for their reproductions of classical architecture models.

MATERIALS AND TECHNIQUES

Doerner, Max. *The Materials of the Artist and Their Use in Painting: With Notes on the Techniques of the Old Masters.* Rev. ed. New York: Harvest Books, 1984.
Technical and craft-related problems of fine art production are discussed extensively in a praxis-oriented manner.

Wehlte, Kurt. *The Materials and Techniques of Painting.* New York: Van Nostrand Reinhold, 1982.
Technical foundations, materials, and techniques of panel and mural painting are treated precisely and extensively.

SOME CONTEMPORARY ARTISTS

Gottfried Böhm, Bauten und Projekte, Auszug aus den Jahren 1995–2000 (Buildings and projects, selections from the years 1995–2000). (German/English.) Tübingen, Berlin: Ernst Wasmuth Verlag, 2000.
A selection of the latest works of the internationally renowned architect and Pritzker Architecture

Prize laureate. *Excellent representations of original models, sketches, and photographs.*

Dehlinger, Laurence. *Die zeitgenössischen Deckenbilder im Schloss Charlottenburg und ihre Folgen* (Contemporary ceiling murals in the Charlottenburg Palace and results). Berlin: Gebrüder Mann, 1997.
Detailed reports on the work of the Berlin architects Peter Schubert, Hann Trier, and other contemporary artists.

Haas, Richard. *The City Is My Canvas*. Munich: Prestel, 2001.
Overview of the impressive work of Richard Haas, who has set new standards for the design of large-format façades since the seventies.

Rust, Graham. *The Painted House. Over 100 Original Designs for Mural and Trompe-L'Oeil Decoration*. Bulfinch, 1997.
This collection of designs enjoys popularity world wide.

163 Playful wall treatment with architectural elements and plants. (Yannick Guégan)

Directory of Artists

The authors thank all the artists who have contributed to this book. (The numbers in parentheses refer to illustrations).

Amblard, Pascal, Paris, France, E-mail: amblard.pascal @wanadoo.fr (5, 93, 94, 128, 150)

Arnild, Susan, Gravlev Bygade 1, 8400 Ebeltoft, Denmark, Tel. +45/86 33/61 38 (53, 55)

Benad, Ursula and Martin, Wörthstraße 25, 81667 Munich, Gemany, Tel. +49/89/4895 1312, www. atelier-benad.de (front cover, frontispiece, 3, 22, 23, 38, 56, 84, 97, 98, 103, 108, 124, 126, 135, 136, 144, 151, 157, 159)

Berghuis Jr., Jan, House of Bendhor-le Fay, Prins Hendrikstraat 84, 2518 HV's-Gravenhage, Netherlands, Tel. +31/70/3601 242 (39, 40, 50, 51, 52)

Biswanger, Claus D., Fürstenstraße 9, 80333 Munich, Germany, Tel. +49/89/282 193 www.illusions-wandmalerei.de (4, 6, 87–89, 91, 138)

Bobin, Jean-Claude, 106, avenue Félix Faure, 92000 Nanterre, France, Tel. +33/141/382 561 (149, 152, 154)

Böhm, Gottfried (10, 90, 109)

Cepiade, Centre pictoral des arts décoratifs, 14 boulevard Jean Jaurès, 92100 Boulogne Billancourt, France, Tel. +33/146/840 060, www.cepiade.com (49, 85)

Deblaere, René, J. en M. Sabbe Straat 10, 8930 Menen, Belgium (48, 81)

Fabienne Colin, Atelier, 14 rue Paul Bert, 94110 Arcueil, France, Tel. +33/1/4985 9458 (114, 156)

Finkelstein, Pierre, Grand Illusion Decorative Painting, Inc., 20 West 20th Street, Suite #1009, New York, N.Y. 10011, www.pfinkelstein.com (41, 42, 47, 57, 72)

Francis, Ron, PO Box 268 Macclesfield, South Australia 5153, http://users.senet.com.au/~rfrancis (100–102, 141–143)

Guégan, Yannick, 61 rue de Hoëdic, 44420 Quimiac – Mesquer, France, Tel. +33/621 01/14 44 (115, 118, 163)

Haas, Richard, 361 W. 36th Street, New York, N.Y. 10018, www.richardhaas.com (8, 106, 122, 123, 158)

Haubitz + Zoche, Georgenstraße 65, 80799 Munich, Germany, E-mail: mail@haubitz-zoche.de (145, 146)

IPEDEC, Institut Supérieur de Peinture Décorative de Paris, 22 rue des Grilles, 93500 Pantin, France, www.ipedec.com

Kreitz, Patrice, 37 rue des Moulins à Vent, 95470 St. Witz, France (43)

Latzke, Rainer Maria, RML Design AG, Bavaria-Film-Platz 3, D-82031 Grünwald, Germany (20, 119, 125, 153)

Müller, Susanne, Weltistraße 57, 81477 Munich, Germany, Tel. +49/89/790 2878 and +49/175/ 5647430, www.traumdesign.com (92, 104, 105, 110)

Moroni, Lucretia, Fatto a Mano by Lucretia Moroni Ltd., 127 Madison Avenue, 4th floor, New York, N.Y. 10016, Tel. +1/212/686 4848, www.netcom. com/~lucet (9, 61, 62)

Murs Dec, École d'Enseignement Professionnel de la Peinture Décorative et Artistique, 11 rue Monteil, 44000 Nantes, France, www.mursdec.com (99)

Nadaï, Michel, The Nadaï-Verdon Advanced School of Decorative Painting, 10 rue du 14 Juillet, 47140 Penne-D'Agenais, France, www.artisans-d-art.com/ trompe-l-oeil (46, 80)

Ohst, Rolf, Am Eichberg 3, 23758 Wangels, Germany, Tel. +49/4382/1352 (11, 37, 113, 120, 121, 161)

Palm Fine Arts, Södra Promenaden 39, 602 34 Norrköping, Sweden, Tel. +46/11/36 6950, www. palmfinearts.nu (96)

Pertl, Thomas, Ahornweg 7, 83129 Höslwang, Germany, www.mensch-farbe-raum.de (21)

Rampp, Karl, 6672 Nesselwängle 118, Austria, Tel. +43/5675/81 88, www.rampp.at (1, 12, 63, 107, 112, 160)

Rust, Graham, The Old Rectory, Somerton, Suffolk IP29 4ND, England (7, 19, 60, 83, 117)

Schubert, Peter (147)

Schwarz, Christoph, Thalkirchner Straße 80, 80337 Munich, Germany, Tel./Fax +49/89/534 965, www. fresken.de (34)

Simonis, Prof. Dr. Arch. Giovanni, piazzale Giulio Cesare 15, 20145 Milan, Italy (86)

Vigini, Nicola, Vigini Studios Inc., 703 Ave. B, San Antonio, Texas 78215, Tel. +1/877/977 3289, www. viginistudios.com (95, 132)

White, Jeanne, 16 rue Diderot, 78100 St. Germain en Laye, France (54, 140)